MARVIN'S ROOM was produced by Playwrights Horizons (Andre Bishop, Artistic Director), in New York City, on November 15, 1991. It was directed by David Petrarca; the set design was by Linda Buchanan; the costume design was by Claudia Boddy; the lighting design was by Robert Christen; the music composition and sound design were by Rob Milburn and the production stage manager was Roy Harris. The cast was as follows:

BESSIE .... Laura Esterman
DR. WALLY .... Tim Monsion
RUTH .... Alice Drummond
BOB .... Tom Aulino
LEE .... Lisa Emery
DR. CHARLOTTE/RETIREMENT
     DIRECTOR .... Shona Tucker
HANK .... Mark Rosenthal
CHARLIE .... Karl Maschek
MARVIN .... Adam Chapnick

MARVIN'S ROOM was originally developed with the assistance of the Victory Gardens Theatre, in Chicago, Illinois. The play was originally produced by the Goodman Theatre, in Chicago, Illinois, in February, 1990. It was further developed and produced by the Hartford Stage Company, in Hartford, Connecticut, in November, 1990.

CHARACTERS

BESSIE, 40 years
DOCTOR WALLY
RUTH, Bessie's aunt, 70 years
BOB, Dr. Wally's brother and receptionist
LEE, Bessie's sister, late 30s
DOCTOR CHARLOTTE
HANK, Lee's 17-year-old son
CHARLIE, Hank's younger brother
RETIREMENT HOME DIRECTOR
MARVIN, Bessie's father

TIME

The present.

PLACE

Various locations in Florida and a mental institution in Ohio.

MARVIN'S ROOM

BY SCOTT McPHERSON

★

★

DRAMATISTS
PLAY SERVICE
INC.

SPECIAL NOTE

Anyone receiving permission to produce MARVIN'S ROOM is required to give
credit to the Author as sole and exclusive Author of the Play on the title page of all
programs distributed in connection with performances of the Play and in all
instances in which the title of the Play appears for purposes of advertising,
publicizing or otherwise exploiting the Play and/or a production thereof. The
name of the Author must appear on a separate line, in which no other name
appears, immediately beneath the title and in size of type equal to 50% of the size
of the largest, most prominent letter used for the title of the Play. No person, firm
or entity may receive credit larger or more prominent than that accorded the Author.

MARVIN'S ROOM

ACT ONE

Scene 1

A doctor's examining room. Bessie, a woman of 40 years, sits. Dr. Wally is seated next to her. He holds a syringe.

BESSIE.   I suppose I should tell you needles bother me a little.

DR. WALLY.   Oh, *(He shudders.)* I know what you mean. All right Augustina, could you give me your arm please? Do you mind if I call you Augustina?

BESSIE.   Well, my name is Bessie.

DR. WALLY.   Bessie. Of course. I'm sorry. Things have been a bit hectic around here. Dr. Serat is away on vacation and this morning our receptionist quit. Usually Nurse Abrams would draw the blood for any blood tests but ... where'd I put the whatchamacallit? The uh, do you see it?

BESSIE.   What?

DR. WALLY.   You know, that um, um, I tie it around your arm to make your veins pop out.

BESSIE.   Tourniquet?

DR. WALLY.   Yes, that's it. Oh, I'm sitting on it. How'd that happen? Okay, give me your arm please.

BESSIE.   Janine quit?

DR. WALLY.   Uh-huh. Did you know her?

BESSIE.   Only from here. I bring my father Marvin and my Aunt Ruth in quite a bit to see Dr. Serat. Why did she quit?

Is she getting married?

DR. WALLY.   No, no. Unbeknownst to any of us she was harboring a deep-seated phobia about cockroaches. She said she just couldn't work here any longer. It made her itch.

BESSIE.   *(Looks around.)* Oh?

DR. WALLY.   I think I have seen you out front. Is your father fairly thin?

BESSIE.   Dad's a bone. You could snap him like a twig.

DR. WALLY.   He's somewhat pale?

BESSIE.   He's as white as a bedsheet unless he's choking. Then he gets a little color.

DR. WALLY.   He has trouble breathing?

BESSIE.   No. He likes to put things in his mouth. I'll walk into his bedroom and he'll be lying there all blue in the face with the Yahtzee dice stuck down his throat. Do you know that game?

DR. WALLY.   Yes.

BESSIE.   It's a fun game, isn't it?

DR. WALLY.   Yes.

BESSIE.   Except Dad sucked all the ink off the dice so it's hard to tell what you're rolling.

DR. WALLY.   And your aunt, now this is odd, but I remember she kept staring at my shoes.

BESSIE.   Ruth has three collapsed vertebrae in her back.

DR. WALLY.   Oh, I'm sorry.

BESSIE.   I'm always lugging one of them in here for something or other.

DR. WALLY.   I hope they are both all right for the moment.

BESSIE.   Oh, they're fine. Dad's dying but he's been dying for about twenty years. He's doing it real slow so I don't miss anything. And Dr. Serat has worked a miracle with Ruth. She's had constant pain from her back since she was born, and now the doctor had her get an electronic anesthetizer, you know, they put the wires right into the brain and when she has a bad pain she just turns her dial. It really is a miracle.

DR. WALLY.   That's wonderful.

BESSIE.   If she uses it in the kitchen our automatic garage

6

door goes up. But that's a small price to pay, don't you think?

DR. WALLY. *(He begins to tie the tourniquet on her arm.)* It's amazing what they can do.

BESSIE. When does Dr. Serat get back from his trip?

DR. WALLY. Not till the end of the month. I'll have to hire a new receptionist without him.

BESSIE. What will you do about the bugs?

DR. WALLY. Bugs? Oh no, we don't have any bugs. That's the thing. It must have all been in her mind. She saw bugs everywhere. Granted there are bugs everywhere in Florida, but none in these offices. *(He sets up some vials.)*

BESSIE. Are those all for me?

DR. WALLY. These here, I have a few in my pocket, and I'll have to scrape up a couple more out of one of these drawers.

BESSIE. That seems like a lot of blood.

DR. WALLY. Well, June, if it seems like a lot of blood, that's because it is. So if you're feeling anxious because we're drawing a lot of blood, you should. So, what you're feeling is perfectly normal.

BESSIE. Bessie.

DR. WALLY. I'm sorry?

BESSIE. My name is Bessie.

DR. WALLY. Did I call you Augustina?

BESSIE. You called me June.

DR. WALLY. I did?

BESSIE. You're confusing me with your other patients.

DR. WALLY. No, I'm not.

BESSIE. You called me June.

DR. WALLY. June is the name of my dog. So why don't we get this over with. Where are the um, the uh ...

BESSIE. What?

DR. WALLY. *(He pulls out a bag of cotton balls.)* Here they are. The bag is sealed so they're still sterile. *(He opens the bag with his teeth.)*

BESSIE. How many days are left in this month? Maybe I should wait.

DR. WALLY. Well, let me find my um, my um, date thing.

BESSIE. Calendar?

DR. WALLY. Twenty-eight days.

BESSIE. I think I'll wait. It's just a vitamin deficiency, right?

DR. WALLY. I said it might be a vitamin deficiency. That is one, and the most probable, explanation for your fatigue and easy bruising. But we must rule out the other possibilities or we're not doing our job. And I wouldn't want Dr. Serat to think I'm neglecting his patients while he's away. Now this will only take a second. *(Bessie extends her arm. He positions the needle.)*

BESSIE. I might pass out.

DR. WALLY. Would you rather lie down?

BESSIE. No. Now that I said it out loud I should be fine. I give Dad shots all the time. *(She pulls away again.)*

DR. WALLY. You know, when I was young and my doctor had to give me an ouch of some sort, he would tell me to look at the pattern on the linoleum floor, squint my eyes, and tell him what pictures I could make out of it. The ouch was over before I knew it.

BESSIE. That's real cute.

DR. WALLY. Why don't you try it?

BESSIE. I don't have your imagination.

DR. WALLY. *(Reaches behind her to get the needle from the cart.)* Just look at the floor and tell me what you see. *(Bessie sees what he is up to and he turns her head back out front.)* Just look at the floor and tell me what you see.

BESSIE. I see a big fat cockroach.

DR. WALLY. Where?

BESSIE. There. *(Dr. Wally tries to step on it. Misses. Tries again. Grabs a magazine and hits it under the cart.)*

DR. WALLY. That wasn't a cockroach.

BESSIE. What was it?

DR. WALLY. From the way it burst, I'd say some sort of bloodsucker.

BESSIE. I think I would like to lie down.

DR. WALLY. I'll see if the room is free. *(Exits. Bessie sits alone for a moment. She then raises her skirt to examine a deep bruise on her thigh. Reenters.)* Nurse Abrams is still in there with a patient.

BESSIE.   Let's just get it over with.

VOICE OF NURSE.   Doctor?!

DR. WALLY.   Excuse me. Would you like a magazine? *(He offers her the magazine that he killed the bug with.)*

BESSIE.   I'm fine. *(Doctor exits.)*

DR. WALLY.   *(Reenters.)* Well ... *(Pause.)* The room is free now.

BESSIE.   That's all right. I'll sit. *(Blackout.)*

Scene 2

Bessie's home. Marvin lies in a bed upstage, barely visible through a wall of glass bricks. Ruth, a woman of 70 years with a slight hunchback, sleeps in a chair. Bessie enters with groceries. Her arms are bruised from the Doctor's attempts to draw blood.

BESSIE.   Aunt Ruth? Ruth?

RUTH.   Hmmmmm.

BESSIE.   Ruth, you're not supposed to sleep sitting in a chair, honey. It puts too much pressure on your lower spine.

RUTH.   You're home.

BESSIE.   Do you want to go lie down?

RUTH.   Don't you look pretty.

BESSIE.   Do you want to lie down?

RUTH.   No, no. Don't you bother about me, now. I'm just fine.

BESSIE.   You're sleeping in the chair.

RUTH.   I am?

BESSIE.   You were, when I came in. That's not good for you.

RUTH.   Oh stupid me. You tell me right away when I'm sleeping because I don't always know.

BESSIE.   I just got home. I couldn't tell you sooner.

RUTH. Look, this control box pulled my sweater. I'm going to have a hole there. It's my own fault.

BESSIE. How's Dad?

RUTH. What did the doctor say?

BESSIE. Oh, he made a big to-do so I wouldn't feel like he was overcharging me.

RUTH. He's a nice man, isn't he. He has very handsome hands.

BESSIE. It wasn't Dr. Serat.

RUTH. Bessie, oh, what happened to your arms?

BESSIE. They took a little blood.

RUTH. It looks tender. Should you see a doctor?

BESSIE. I just came from the doctor.

RUTH. Did you show him your arms?

BESSIE. Yes, he just had some trouble finding my veins.

RUTH. That sounds serious.

BESSIE. I have a vitamin deficiency, Ruth, that's all.

RUTH. It's because you don't make stinky often enough.

BESSIE. I do so.

RUTH. Stinky is poison. You have to get rid of it. That's why when you're constipated you have a headache.

BESSIE. *(She picks up Marvin's pills.)* Did you give Dad his five o'clock?

RUTH. What did I do? What time is it now?

BESSIE. Five twenty-five.

RUTH. No, but I was going to.

BESSIE. Honey, I asked you to do one thing.

RUTH. I'm so stupid. I'm useless, I know.

BESSIE. You are not.

RUTH. It's my cure, I think. It's because I have these wires in my brain.

BESSIE. It's not your cure. You blame your cure for everything.

RUTH. I can feel them. They tingle when I bathe.

BESSIE. You used to blame your pain, now you blame your cure.

RUTH. It's gotten so I'm afraid to get in the tub.

BESSIE. You've always been afraid to get in the tub.

RUTH.   Oh, no, no, no. I've never been afraid to get in the tub.

BESSIE.   You make me come in and towel down the floor.

RUTH.   That's because I'm afraid to get out of the tub. The floor gets so wet. Do you remember Mrs. Steingetz fell and the poor thing cracked her head wide open. No one found her until her family came down for Thanksgiving, and even then not until the end of their visit.

BESSIE.   I remember.

RUTH.   She'd still be there if they hadn't run out of towels in the guest bath.

BESSIE.   I know.

RUTH.   I don't want to be lying on the tiles till the holiday season.

BESSIE.   You won't.

RUTH.   I mean, my goodness, it's only just June.

BESSIE.   I hope you remembered to give Dad his four o'clock.

RUTH.   Oh, stupid me.

BESSIE.   Ruth, he is supposed to get his pills at the same time every day.

RUTH.   I know but —

BESSIE.   You never forget to watch your program, do you? You never forget what time your show comes on.

RUTH.   You usually give Marvin his pills.

BESSIE.   Today I asked you to. *(Bessie goes into Marvin's room to give him his pills while Ruth crosses to the kitchen to get her vitamins. From Marvin's room.)* I have been running all over today. Would you quit hogging the bed so I can sit down. Here. Take these now. We're a little off schedule today. Have you been pulling at your sheets? You've got them all twisted. That can't be very comfortable. What does that face mean? Mr. Innocent. How about some tomato soup? And some juice? Water? Juice? Which? Juice. *(Reenters.)* He's confused. He doesn't know why he's getting his four o'clock at five thirty.

RUTH.   *(With pills.)* Do you want to take one of mine for your deficiency?

BESSIE.   I'll get some real vitamins later.

RUTH. These are real. They're just easier to swallow because I don't like to swallow things. Do you want Pebbles or Bam-Bam?
BESSIE. Ruth.
RUTH. Dino came out.
BESSIE. Dino's fine.
RUTH. Chew it up good. We have to take care of you, too. *(Slight pause.)* That cat came around today.
BESSIE. Honey, it's just a little kitty. It won't bother you.
RUTH. It came right up to the house and stared in at me. It sat there like it was stone.
BESSIE. Uh-huh.
RUTH. What do you think it wants?
BESSIE. I don't think it wants anything.
RUTH. I know you have things you have to do and it's hard getting someone to come in but I wish you wouldn't leave me at home alone.
BESSIE. Honey, you do fine.
RUTH. But I'm so useless. What if Marvin were to choke on something again? What if he gets hold of the Yahtzee dice or tries to kill himself with the Parcheesi men?
BESSIE. Dr. Serat explained this to you. He puts things in his mouth because it gives him pleasure. He likes the way it feels. You know how much he likes it when you bounce the light off your compact mirror? This is another thing he likes. He's not trying to choke himself.
RUTH. What if he dies while you're out of the house?
BESSIE. Then you'll call me and I'll come home. *(Pause.)* You've got your cure now. There's no reason you can't help out around here. I don't ask you to do much.
RUTH. Do you want me to make the tomato soup?
BESSIE. No. You'd make a mess of it. *(She starts to make the soup.)*
RUTH. I'll go bounce the light around Marvin's room.
BESSIE. That's a good idea. Why don't you do that. And later we'll watch some TV. All right?
RUTH. All right. *(She goes into Marvin's room.)*
BESSIE. *(Pouring a can of soup into a metal pan.)* Do you re-

member all the foods Dad used to like. Flapjacks and bacon and eggs — *(Ruth moves her mirror above Marvin's bed and the light starts dancing on the wall of his room.)* — and grits and biscuits and roast beef and green beans and mashed potatoes and apple pie and ice cream he churned himself. *(Lights fade to black. The bouncing light in Marvin's room is the last to go out.)*

Scene 3

The doctor's office. Bessie sits alone.

DR. WALLY.   *(Enters with a bicycle wheel.)* I'm sorry to have kept you waiting.

BESSIE.   You must be very busy.

DR. WALLY.   But I couldn't find a place to lock my bike.

BESSIE.   Oh.

DR. WALLY.   Well, how are we today?

BESSIE.   You tell me.

DR. WALLY.   That's a pretty dress you're wearing. Is it new?

BESSIE.   It's the same one I always wear into town.

DR. WALLY.   Well, I can see why.

BESSIE.   I suppose it can't be good news or you would have just told me over the phone.

DR. WALLY.   Your um ... your um ...

BESSIE.   Blood test.

DR. WALLY.   It's our policy not to give any test results over the phone.

BESSIE.   Oh. Because I really got myself worked up. I was thinking all sorts of horrible thoughts.

DR. WALLY.   I certainly didn't mean to worry you. But I did think it would be a good idea for me to see you again.

BESSIE.   Oh? *(The phone rings.)*

DR. WALLY.   *(Answers it.)* Dr. Wally speaking. Yes, I know I have someone waiting in my office. I am in my office. That's all right. *(Hangs up.)*

BESSIE.   Is there a problem?

DR. WALLY.   No. He's just new. He'll get the hang of it.

BESSIE.   I meant with my blood test. Did it get lost or something?

DR. WALLY.   No, no. It didn't get lost. But I would like to run some other tests.

BESSIE.   Oh, you would?

DR. WALLY.   Simply to rule out certain possibilities.

BESSIE.   Uh-huh.

DR. WALLY.   We could take the sample now if you have the time.

BESSIE.   What are the possibilities?

DR. WALLY.   There are a number of possibilities I would like to rule out.

BESSIE.   Are you still thinking I have a vitamin deficiency?

DR. WALLY.   I think we may have ruled out that possibility.

BESSIE.   Do you think we should? Should we rule that out?

DR. WALLY.   Why don't we take this sample and then we'll have a better idea of what we're talking about. *(Pause.)*

BESSIE.   I left Aunt Ruth in charge of Dad. I shouldn't be gone long.

DR. WALLY.   This won't take long. *(Pause. Bessie puts her arm out.)* That won't be necessary.

BESSIE.   Oh. I think I'm too nervous to pee into a cup.

DR. WALLY.   There's no reason to be nervous. What I am going to do is this. I am going to give you a local anesthetic and then I'm going to remove a little bone marrow from your hip.

BESSIE.   What?

DR. WALLY.   You won't really feel it. Maybe a slight pinching. Now, it will make a little noise so don't let that bother you.

BESSIE.   You're going to take bone marrow out of my hip?

DR. WALLY.   Just a little. There will be a crunching noise. If you've ever had your wisdom teeth pulled you know the sound. And you also know that it sounds worse than it is.

BESSIE.   I've never had my wisdom teeth out.

DR. WALLY.   Really. Hmmmm. Maybe you should see someone.

BESSIE. I've never had a problem with them.

DR. WALLY. Good teeth are a blessing. I've never had a cavity in my life.

BESSIE. I've had my share I guess.

DR. WALLY. I'm no dentist but as you get older cavities aren't so much the problem. It's gum disease.

BESSIE. I always massage my gums and I brush my tongue.

DR. WALLY. Do you floss?

BESSIE. Not as often as I should.

DR. WALLY. Who does? Could you hike up your dress, please?

BESSIE. I don't mean to be nosy, but could you tell me why you're going to take bone marrow out of my hip?

DR. WALLY. There's not a lot of flesh on the hip.

BESSIE. But what is the test for?

DR. WALLY. Why don't you let me do the worrying for now?

BESSIE. I am probably thinking it's something much worse than it actually is.

DR. WALLY. I wouldn't waste your time thinking anything until we get the test results back.

BESSIE. Is it serious like a brain tumor?

DR. WALLY. No, no.

BESSIE. M.S.?

DR. WALLY. No.

BESSIE. Cancer? *(Pause.)* Cancer?

DR. WALLY. *(Picks up the phone.)* Hold my calls please. *(Hangs up.)* Bessie — *(The phone rings. He answers.)* Dr. Wally speaking. Yes, that was me just then. Didn't you recognize my voice? You can tell by which little light blinks on your phone. That's all right. *(Hangs up.)* That's what I get for hiring my own brother. Bessie, first I should explain your blood test.

BESSIE. Okay.

DR. WALLY. You have something on your shoulder.

BESSIE. I do?

DR. WALLY. It's a button.

BESSIE. Is that bad?

DR. WALLY. No, it's part of your dress. I thought it was a

bug. Believe it or not we are having something of a problem with them after all. I'm not doing this very well.

BESSIE. Should I be worried?

DR. WALLY. No. Would you like a cup of coffee?

BESSIE. I'd love one.

DR. WALLY. *(Picks up his phone.)* This is Dr. Wally speaking. Please bring a cup of coffee to my office. *(Hangs up.)*

BESSIE. Could it have to do with whether or not I poo regularly?

DR. WALLY. We'll want to look at everything. But your blood work shows abnormally low levels of red cells, platelets and mature white cells.

BESSIE. I haven't felt as bad lately. I haven't been nearly as tired.

DR. WALLY. That's good. Now, your spleen and your liver, on your last visit, felt slightly enlarged.

BESSIE. Is that bad?

DR. WALLY. Well, one of the possibilities that I am hoping to rule out is leukemia. *(Pause.)*

BESSIE. Uh-huh. *(The phone rings.)*

DR. WALLY. I don't have to answer it.

BESSIE. Pick it up.

DR. WALLY. *(Answers phone.)* This is Dr. Wally speaking. *(He cups the receiver and speaks to Bessie.)* Do you take cream?

BESSIE. Yes.

DR. WALLY. Yes. And don't call me anymore, Bob. I mean it. *(Hangs up.)*

BESSIE. Odds are it's leukemia, right?

DR. WALLY. Odds don't mean anything. I could tell you that, yes, with your symptoms and your blood work the odds favor leukemia, but that doesn't mean anything. You're an individual not a statistic.

BESSIE. But they do?

DR. WALLY. This is why I was reluctant to — . You are worried now and you may not have cause to be.

BESSIE. What does it mean if it is leukemia?

DR. WALLY. What do you mean?

BESSIE. Is it still fatal?

DR. WALLY.   What do you mean?

BESSIE.   I mean, does it still kill you?

DR. WALLY.   You must remember there are a variety of leukemias and a variety of treatments. Radiation therapy, chemotherapy. Bone-marrow transplants, which a few years ago were considered experimental, are now a very real option. You do have family?

BESSIE.   Dad and Ruth.

DR. WALLY.   No other?

BESSIE.   No.

DR. WALLY.   Are you sure?

BESSIE.   Yes.

DR. WALLY.   I thought your file mentioned a sister.

BESSIE.   Oh. Yes. I have a sister. Lee. Yes.

DR. WALLY.   Well, we're getting a little ahead of ourselves anyway. No one said you had leukemia so it's premature to talk of treatment options.

BESSIE.   So you think I'm overreacting?

DR. WALLY.   I understand your reaction.

BESSIE.   My mother had leukemia.

DR. WALLY.   I know.

BESSIE.   You know?

DR. WALLY.   Why don't we take this sample and you can get home to your father and your aunt.

BESSIE.   All right. *(Bob enters.)*

BOB.   Coffee?

BESSIE.   Oh, thank you. *(She takes the coffee. Bob exits. Dr. Wally raises her dress. Bessie doesn't know what to do with the coffee.)*

DR. WALLY.   You can drink your coffee. *(Bessie, standing, rapidly sips the too-hot coffee from the white styrofoam cup. The Doctor, standing, needle in hand, waits. The lights fade to black as Bessie repeatedly sips.)*

Scene 4

The visiting room of a mental institution in Ohio. There are three chairs. Dr. Charlotte sits in one. Lee, a woman in her late 30s, sits in another.

LEE.   Do you mind if I smoke?

DR. CHARLOTTE.   Yes. Thank you for asking.

LEE.   How 'bout I blow it this way?

DR. CHARLOTTE.   I'm afraid there's no smoking anywhere on this floor.

LEE.   I'll be very quiet then. *(She lights up. Pause. She looks at her watch.)* I should have called, right?

DR. CHARLOTTE.   They're getting him. He's in occupational therapy which is in another building on the grounds.

LEE.   Oh, I see.

DR. CHARLOTTE.   It's good to see you here, Lee. May I call you Lee?

LEE.   Sure.

DR. CHARLOTTE.   We've missed you on other days, so has Hank.

LEE.   I know. I wish I could visit more but ... well ... you know.

DR. CHARLOTTE.   Mm-hmm.

LEE.   Now, you're not an orderly are you?

DR. CHARLOTTE.   I'm a psychiatrist.

LEE.   Are you who Hank talks to?

DR. CHARLOTTE.   I'm in charge of his therapy. He talks to me and others on staff.

LEE.   Well, you know he lies. I'm just telling you that, I mean not because I think he's been saying bad things about me, but I'm sure he has been. I mean I'm sure he has been. But you should know he lies to help you with his therapy.

DR. CHARLOTTE.   Mm-hmm.

LEE.   For instance he told his guidance counselor at school that I beat him.

18

DR. CHARLOTTE.   Mm-hmm.

LEE.   So you see what I mean.

DR. CHARLOTTE.   Mm-hmm.

LEE.   Oh, see now, you're thinking, oh, I wonder if she does beat him.

DR. CHARLOTTE.   Is that what you think I think?

LEE.   Don't you?

DR. CHARLOTTE.   Do you want me to think that?

LEE.   What do you mean?

DR. CHARLOTTE.   What do you think I mean?

LEE.   What do you mean, what do I think you mean?

DR. CHARLOTTE.   What do you think I mean by what do you think I mean? *(Pause.)*

LEE.   You wouldn't have an ashtray, would you? *(Dr. Charlotte takes a glass ashtray out and crosses to her.)* Do you want a drag? *(Pause.)*

DR. CHARLOTTE.   No. Here. *(She hands the ashtray to Lee.)* We'd like to have you become more involved in Hank's therapy. We'd like you to come more often for visits.

LEE.   Doctor, can I be honest with you? What is your first name?

DR. CHARLOTTE.   Charlotte.

LEE.   Oh, my youngest boy's a Charlie.

DR. CHARLOTTE.   Yes.

LEE.   Charlotte. I've forced myself through school and I'm about to get my degree. I'm very picky now about the kind of man I'll go with. I keep — I used to keep a very clean house. Hank makes fun of my degree in cosmetology. He terrorizes any man I'm interested in. This last one, Lawrence, Hank made fun of his being on parole, made fun of the way he held his liquor, made fun of his Pinto. The point is, Hank cost me a potentially good relationship. And as for my house.... Hank is not something I can control so what is the point of my visiting?

DR. CHARLOTTE.   He says he misses you. *(Hank enters. He is a big 17-year-old covered with motor grease.)*

HANK.   Hey.

LEE.   Look at you. You look like a pig.

HANK. I'm working on an engine.

LEE. Don't they let you shower?

HANK. They told me you were here and I was supposed to come here.

LEE. Don't sit down, Hank. *(He sits.)* You'll get the chair all greasy. *(Slight pause.)* Are you behaving yourself?

HANK. They're not strapping me down anymore.

LEE. Well, don't abuse that privilege. You want an M&M? I got some in my purse.

HANK. Where's Charlie? He didn't come?

LEE. He has a class in geometry.

HANK. He's already taken remedial geometry.

LEE. This is a makeup class in remedial geometry. *(To Dr. Charlotte.)* Charlie's not doing too well in school.

DR. CHARLOTTE. Mm-hmm.

LEE. They say it's because he reads too much. Do you want — *(Offers M&M.)*

DR. CHARLOTTE. No, thank you.

LEE. So, are you behaving yourself?

HANK. I told you yes.

LEE. All right, I'm just asking.

HANK. So how come you're visiting?

LEE. What do you mean? I don't have to have a reason to visit.

HANK. Then how come you've never visited before?

LEE. I have visited before but you were unconscious.

HANK. That doesn't count as a visit. How can it be a visit if I didn't know you were here?

LEE. I can't be responsible for when you're conscious or unconscious, I can only make the effort.

DR. CHARLOTTE. Mm-hmm.

LEE. Maybe if I knew you were going to be conscious for sure I would visit more often. Do you have some sort of schedule I could take with me?

DR. CHARLOTTE. Your son is off the Thorazine now. You should find him alert most any visiting day.

LEE. See, that's another thing. Saturdays are just about the worst for me. We're still living in the basement of the church because of our house, and on Saturday I help the nuns; since they took us in I feel I should do something around the place.

DR. CHARLOTTE.   Mm-hmm.

LEE.   On Saturdays the nuns roll out a sheet of dough and with this shot glass they cut out the, what do you call it, the body-of-Christ thing they use for their Communion. Now I'm not allowed to actually touch the dough because I'm not a Catholic, but I make sure there's lots of flour spread out on the table so the body-of-Christ thing doesn't stick because it's hell to clean up. You end up having to scrape it with your nails. And I keep count of how many bodies-of-Christ things they've made.

DR. CHARLOTTE.   Communion Hosts.

LEE.   That's right. It's very relaxing. All the girls get to talking. (*Hank crosses to leave. Dr. Charlotte stops him and sits him down.*)

DR. CHARLOTTE.   Do you think the nuns would understand if you told them you needed to come visit your son?

LEE.   I'm here today, aren't I?

DR. CHARLOTTE.   Yes.   ·

LEE.   (*Offering Hank an M&M.*) I did come up here to tell you something — (*She puts it in his mouth.*) your hands are too greasy — though I was planning on coming today anyway.

HANK.   What?

LEE.   Well, now, it's not good news but your doctor thinks it's all right to tell you because, partially, I've got no choice.

HANK.   What?

LEE.   You know your Aunt Bessie down in Florida. Well, she's got leukemia and I guess she's not doing too well and there's a possibility she might die.

HANK.   Who?

LEE.   Your Aunt Bessie.

HANK.   I didn't know I had an Aunt Bessie.

LEE.   Sure you did. My sister. Your aunt. She lives down in Florida.

HANK.   This is the first I've heard of her.

LEE.   She's been to the house.

HANK.   When?

LEE.   Right after your dad and I got married.

HANK.   I wasn't born yet.

LEE.   Oh, I guess you weren't. Well I know I've mentioned her. She's my sister.

HANK.   I didn't know you had a sister.

LEE.   You know how at Christmas I always say, it looks like Bessie didn't send a card this year either.

HANK.   Oh yeah.

LEE.   That's your Aunt Bessie, my sister.

HANK.   Okay.

LEE.   And she's dying.

HANK.   Okay. Are there any more M&Ms?

LEE.   Sure. *(She puts one in his mouth.)* Since we're her nearest relatives they want us to get tested to see if our bone marrow is compatible because they could maybe save her life if they do a bone-marrow transplant.

HANK.   Yeah?

LEE.   They wanted us to fly to Florida but we can't afford that. So we're going to arrange the tests up here and send them down. Okay?

HANK.   Why don't we go to Florida?

LEE.   Because we don't have any money, Hank. It's a really simple test, they say. And it's not supposed to hurt much.

HANK.   What if I don't want to do it?

LEE.   What do you mean?

HANK.   I don't know her. Why should I let them do anything to me?

LEE.   This is my sister we are talking about. And maybe I haven't mentioned her to you before but that doesn't mean that she isn't on my mind a lot and we are not going to just let her die because you want to have one of your moods. Do you understand? Now they say they can do your test up here so ... *(Hank has walked away and turned his back.)* Well, I have to go. It's good to see you, Hank.

HANK.   You coming next week?

LEE.   I don't know. It's Feast of the Ascension. It gets kind of busy.

DR. CHARLOTTE.   Hank, is there anything you want to say to your mother?

LEE.   Will it take long, because I am already late?

HANK.   No, I just — well, I'm really sorry I burnt the house down.

LEE.   Is that it, 'cause I am really late? Okay, Hank. Well you be good now. I'd leave you these but they're Charlie's. I just took them with me for the drive. Here, I'll leave you some here. Then when you get cleaned up you can come back for them. *(She pours out some M&Ms on the seat of the chair.)* Okay, well, we'll see you, and Bessie's doctor should be calling you.

DR. CHARLOTTE.   We'll be waiting. *(Lee exits.)* Well ... *(She takes out a cigarette, lights it and takes a deep drag.)* Good session.

Scene 5

Bessie lies in her hospital bed, wearing a wig and eating lunch. Ruth sits in a chair beside her.

RUTH.   Being confined to your bed is nothing to be afraid of.

BESSIE.   I'm not confined to my bed. I'm just a little tired today.

RUTH.   I was confined to my bed most of my life. You find things to do.

BESSIE.   Like what?

RUTH.   Oh my, well, you can sleep or you can lay there awake ...

BESSIE.   Do you want any of this?

RUTH.   No, no. That's all for you. You eat that and be strong. Have you made a stinky today?

BESSIE.   Yes.

RUTH.   That's good. That's important. Do you want your rice pudding?

BESSIE.   Do you want it?

RUTH. Not if you were going to have it.

BESSIE. You can have it.

RUTH. I didn't really have time for a lunch.

BESSIE. This is too far for you to come, Ruth. I don't think you should visit me again.

RUTH. You visited me every day when I was in for my cure. It's nice for me to visit you.

BESSIE. It's too hard on you.

RUTH. It's such a lovely walk.

BESSIE. Besides, you're needed at home now.

RUTH. I wish we could do something about that garage door. I feel like the whole street knows my business.

BESSIE. How is Dad?

RUTH. Oh, he's fine.

BESSIE. Does he miss me?

RUTH. Well, I haven't actually told him you're gone.

BESSIE. What?

RUTH. I didn't know what to say.

BESSIE. Doesn't he wonder where I am?

RUTH. When he asks I say you're just in the other room busy with something. Then he falls asleep for a while and when he wakes up I say he just missed you.

BESSIE. Ruth.

RUTH. It would upset him.

BESSIE. Who does he think that nurse is living with you?

RUTH. Well, I pretend not to notice her.

BESSIE. What do you mean?

RUTH. If she comes in the room while I'm there I pretend she's not real. That she doesn't exist.

BESSIE. Then what does Dad think?

RUTH. I think he thinks he's hallucinating.

BESSIE. What?

RUTH. I never told him he was hallucinating. He came up with that himself. I didn't know what to do. I was going to try to tell him you were in the hospital and — and she walked in before I was ready so I didn't — I — I pretended she wasn't there.

BESSIE. You have to tell him.

RUTH. But he's used to it now. The only time it seems to bother him is when she carries him to the bath. And I say oh, look Marvin, you're flying. Bessie will want to see this. And I go into the other room to get you.

BESSIE. He must think he's losing his mind.

RUTH. But it's better than telling him. You don't know. He would be so upset. He's still your father. What am I supposed to tell him? That his little girl is — ? How can I tell him? Then he'll really think he's losing his mind. He'll be so upset. It would be so upsetting to him. He's your father.

BESSIE. All right. All right.

RUTH. I wouldn't know what to say.

BESSIE. Tell him that I'm going to be fine and I'll be home soon and there's no reason to be upset.

RUTH. You want me to tell him?

BESSIE. Yes. Because there is no reason to be upset. I'm going to be fine, Ruth. I know I am.

RUTH. Nothing happens that God doesn't have a reason for.

BESSIE. I'm sure He does.

RUTH. He tries to teach us things. He tries to reach down and shake us out of our ignorance.

BESSIE. I'm sure that's it.

RUTH. I know He made me crippled for a reason. He wants me to learn something. It may be patience or it may be forbearance or it may be how to dress without standing up. He doesn't tell you what it is, you just have to learn it.

BESSIE. I don't think it's how to dress.

RUTH. Oh, it wouldn't surprise me. I often ask Him why I'm crippled. I also ask Him why he let Marvin buy this house down here to take care of me then struck Marvin with a stroke. Why? And then have him lose his colon to cancer. Why? And then lose the sight in one eye and the use of one kidney and yet keep a full head of hair. Why?

BESSIE. I don't know.

RUTH. But God knows. He has His reasons. And I'm not upset.

BESSIE. Then tell Dad his nurse is not a hallucination and

that I am not in the other room.

RUTH.   I think he's starting to enjoy flying.

BESSIE.   And I don't want you to visit me again. It's too hard on you. *(Pause.)* It's almost time for your show. Don't you want to watch?

RUTH.   I didn't think you would want to.

BESSIE.   I kind of want to see if Lance proposes to Coral.

RUTH.   Have you been watching?

BESSIE.   I've seen it since I've been in here.

RUTH.   *(Sits on the bed with Bessie.)* Isn't it wonderful? I think she'll say yes. They really do love each other.

BESSIE.   But now, is he the same guy who raped her at one point?

RUTH.   Oh, that was months ago. He's really a nice boy. *(Bessie clicks on the TV with the remote. They both look to the corner of the room where the TV would be. The soap-opera theme music swells as the lights fade.)*

Scene 6

Bessie's home. Bessie is in Marvin's room.

BESSIE.   Okay, Dad. Roll that way. Let me get the sheet. Oh, c'mon you can help me out a little bit. *(Doorbell rings. Lee enters with suitcases.)* Ruth! Dad, now I need to get that side of the sheet too so would you roll toward me now. Just a little.

LEE.   Hello?

BESSIE.   Lee?

LEE.   Bessie?

BESSIE.   I'll be right out. *(To Marvin.)* Now you'll be okay for a moment. I've just got to put these to soak. *(Enters carrying balled-up sheets.)* Lee!

LEE.   Bessie. I rang the bell.

BESSIE.   Didn't Ruth let you in?

LEE.   No, she —

BESSIE.   Well, I don't know where she got to. She's probably in front of the TV somewhere. I told her to keep an eye out for you.

LEE. *(Overlapping.)* That's all right. She probably just didn't hear the bell. I just let myself in. I hope you don't mind.

BESSIE. Not at all. Look at you.

LEE. What?

BESSIE. Look at you. Are you that old? How old does that make me, then?

LEE. Why, do I look old?

BESSIE. Well, you're a lot older.

LEE. You look good though, Bessie. You really do. I like your hair.

BESSIE. This is a wig. It's from my chemo.

LEE. Oh. *(Slight pause.)* I know it's a wig. I don't know why I pretended I didn't. Not that it looks like a wig.

BESSIE. Thanks.

LEE. I'm wearing a fall. Isn't that something. I've always loved this length but I've never had the patience for it. I just wear it when I want to look nice.

BESSIE. Why don't you sit down. I've got to put these to soak. Dad had himself a little accident.

LEE. Oh. How is he?

BESSIE. He's still with us.

LEE. Let me help.

BESSIE. No, no. You sit down. This will only take a second. *(Exits.)*

LEE. *(Stands by the entrance to Marvin's room.)* Daddy? It's me, Lee. All the way down from Ohio. We came after all. *(Pause.)* The nuns had a big bake sale for us to pay for our way down here. Can I come in? *(She goes in.)* Hi, Daddy. *(She reenters, slightly upset.)*

BESSIE. *(Reentering.)* I let them soak and worry about them later. Oh, Lee I don't know if you should smoke in the house.

LEE. Oh I'm ...

BESSIE. No, you could smoke in the garage if you ...

LEE. No, no.

BESSIE. Dad's oxygen tanks.

LEE. I understand.

BESSIE. Or you could smoke in the yard ...

LEE. I don't have to smoke.

BESSIE. Where're your boys? Couldn't you get Hank out of the mental institution?

LEE. Bessie, we don't like to call it the mental institution.

BESSIE. What do you call it?

LEE. We call it the loony bin or the nut house to show we've got a sense of humor about it.

BESSIE. Well where is he? Where's Charlie? I've got myself two grown nephews I've never seen.

LEE. Now I invited you up for both their christenings.

BESSIE. I've got my hands full down here.

LEE. Who stayed while you were in the hospital?

BESSIE. We had a nurse come in.

LEE. That must have been expensive. I want to write you a check.

BESSIE. Oh no. That's all right.

LEE. Don't worry. It's not going to be much. *(Writing check.)*

BESSIE. That's okay, Lee. We've gotten by this long. We're glad you're here now.

LEE. Of course I'm here. You're my sister.

BESSIE. Where are your boys?

LEE. They're sitting out in the car.

BESSIE. The car? Why don't they come in?

LEE. You have to ask Hank that.

BESSIE. Do they need help with their stuff?

LEE. He's just doing this to make me mad.

BESSIE. Should we —

LEE. Don't worry about it. I know how to handle Hank. He won't cause you a problem while he's here.

BESSIE. You probably want to see Dad. It's been such a long time.

LEE. Sure.

BESSIE. Well let me get him dressed and cleaned up a little. He wouldn't want you to see him like he is.

LEE. You sure I can't help?

BESSIE. I've been doing it this long. *(Bessie goes into Marvin's*

room. Ruth enters.)
LEE. Aunt Ruth?
RUTH. Oh, look who it is! And isn't she pretty.
LEE. Aunt Ruth?
RUTH. You remember an old thing like me?
LEE. You're up and about.
RUTH. Oh, I've got my cure. I'm part machine. I hope you don't think I'm rude but I'm watching my show and I just hate to miss it. I knew you'd come right when it starts.
LEE. Oh no, you watch your program.
RUTH. Are you going to give me a hug? *(Lee hugs Ruth.)* Give me a real hug. I won't break. *(Lee hugs Ruth harder. This hurts Ruth.)* Oh Jesus. Oh sweet Jesus. Oh Jesus. *(Ruth turns her dial and the garage door is heard going up.)*
LEE. Oh. I'm sorry. I'm sorry. Here sit.
BESSIE. *(Reenters.)* I heard the garage door.
RUTH. Lee hurt my back.
LEE. I didn't mean to.
BESSIE. I'm sure she didn't mean to.
RUTH. I know she didn't mean to. She's a sweet girl.
LEE. I brought some cookies left over from the bake sale.
RUTH. Isn't that thoughtful. But I'm not allowed sugar.
LEE. But you'll like them, Bessie. Seven-layer cookies.
BESSIE. Thanks, Lee, but I'm trying to stay away from that stuff now too.
LEE. Does Dad still have a sweet tooth?
BESSIE. You bet.
LEE. That's good.
BESSIE. Which makes his diabetes all the more frustrating.
LEE. Diabetes?
RUTH. But it's a lovely canister, isn't it.
BESSIE. Do you want to see Dad?
LEE. Sure.
RUTH. Who are those two boys sitting in the car in the driveway?
LEE. That's Hank and Charlie. This is something I need to tell you both.
RUTH. I think the commercial break must be over. Could

you tell me later?

LEE. Oh, sure. *(Ruth exits.)* Bessie, Hank will do things like this to get attention. They say I just have to ignore it. Or give him an ultimatum.

BESSIE. What about Charlie?

LEE. He just goes along with Hank. Or he might be reading.

BESSIE. What if I ask them in?

LEE. No. If we ask them in I have to be prepared to make him come in. I don't feel up to it.

BESSIE. Oh now.

LEE. He just wants the attention. He hasn't agreed to be tested for the transplant yet because he knows he'll be the center of attention. You have to ignore him.

BESSIE. He hasn't?

LEE. Oh, but don't worry. He will.

BESSIE. We can't have him do anything he doesn't want to.

LEE. No. He will. I'll make him if I have to.

BESSIE. How are you going to make him, Lee? You can't make him come in from the drive. *(Pause. Lee exits. Bessie sees the check, picks it up. She tears up the check and puts the pieces back on the counter.)*

RUTH. *(Enters.)* I keep missing the show and only catch the commercials.

BESSIE. You're supposed to watch. You're supposed to tell me what happens.

LEE. *(Reenters.)* Can I use your phone?

BESSIE. Sure.

LEE. Do you have the number for the police?

BESSIE. Why? What happened?

RUTH. *(Simultaneously.)* Oh my!

LEE. Nothing's happened. I had to give Hank an ultimatum. That's what his doctor told me I'm supposed to do. Clearly define the rules so Hank knows what the consequences are.

BESSIE. Couldn't you tell him no more TV?

LEE. He burned the TV.

RUTH. Are they smoking drugs out there?

LEE. Do you have the number?

BESSIE. This seems extreme.

LEE. Just give me the number Bessie.

BESSIE. Here's a list of emergency numbers. It's right there under chicken delivery.

LEE. Thank you. I'm sorry about this. *(She dials.)*

RUTH. Coral told Storm she is going to marry Lance.

BESSIE. Tell me later, Ruth, okay? *(Hank and Charlie enter. Charlie is engrossed in a book.)*

HANK. Hey.

BESSIE. Well look who's here.

LEE. Thank you for coming in, Hank.

HANK. We were coming in Mom. They were doing a top-ten countdown and we wanted to hear number one.

LEE. Why didn't you say that?

HANK. I don't know. You were shouting and everything. It just didn't seem like the time.

LEE. You're trying to make me look bad in front of your aunts and they see right through it.

BESSIE. Well you're here. And I'm your Aunt Bessie who you have never laid eyes on but I don't care if you are all grown up, I expect a big fat hug.

HANK. Sure. *(Hugs Bessie.)*

RUTH. I'm Ruth. *(Hank hugs Ruth.)* Oh Jesus. Oh sweet Jesus. Oh Jesus. *(Ruth turns her dial and the garage door is heard.)*

HANK. What'd I do? What'd I do? I'm sorry. — What's that noise?

RUTH. It's that damn garage. Driving me nuts.

BESSIE. Sit down Ruth.

RUTH. I'm fine.

BESSIE. And you must be Charlie. Do you have a hug for your Aunt Bessie? *(Charlie hugs her.)*

RUTH. And I'm Ruth, your great aunt. *(Charlie extends his hand to her.)* Thank you. Which one of you handsome boys is in the mental institution?

BESSIE. She means the loony bin.

HANK. That's me.

31

BESSIE. Do you all want to go in and see Dad?

HANK. Sure.

RUTH. Marvin! Company's coming! Company's coming!

BESSIE. I know he's excited about meeting all of you. *(They go in. Marvin is heard muttering.)* Dad, it's Lee, your daughter, and these are her boys, your grandkids. No, don't be scared. They're real. They're real. Maybe this is too much right now. *(They leave the room. Ruth stays inside.)*

RUTH. *(From Marvin's room.)* Don't be scared of your own grandkids.

BESSIE. It's just too much excitement.

LEE. Should you be taking it easy?

BESSIE. I'm fine. I seem to be in remission, which is the best time for a transplant. I want to thank you all for coming down here and for helping me out. It's a lot to ask of someone to donate their bone marrow.

CHARLIE. I think it sounds neat.

BESSIE. But I could understand if someone were to be reluctant.

HANK. I'm thinking about it, that's all.

BESSIE. Lee, your appointment is today at three. I hope you don't feel rushed.

LEE. No.

BESSIE. The odds are better that your mother will be a match so she'll get tested first and then maybe you kids won't have to bother.

CHARLIE. *(Disappointed.)* Really? *(Hank picks up a potato chip out of a bowl.)*

LEE. Hank, did Bessie offer you a chip yet?

BESSIE. Oh, that's what they're there for.

LEE. He has to wait to be asked, Bessie. Put the chip back Hank. *(Pause.)* Put it back. *(Pause.)* Put back the chip. *(Pause. Lee crumbles the chip in Hank's hand.)*

BESSIE. Lee, I put them out for the kids.

LEE. You have to understand, he has to wait to be asked.

BESSIE. Hank, would you like a chip?

HANK. No, thank you, Aunt Bessie. Not right now.

LEE. Your aunt offered you a chip, the polite thing to do

would be to take it.

HANK.   I don't want one right now.

LEE.   Eat a chip or no Disney World.

HANK.   I could give a fuck about Disney World.

LEE.   That's it. Get out of my sight. I don't care where. Just so I can't see you. *(Hank exits the house. Pause.)*

BESSIE.   Charlie, would you like a chip? *(Charlie looks at his mom.)*

LEE.   Go ahead honey, if you want one.

BESSIE.   Take a bunch. *(Charlie grabs a handful.)*

LEE.   Not too many. You'll spoil your lunch. *(Charlie puts them all back but one. He is about to bite it.)* Don't make crumbs on your aunt's nice floor. *(Charlie sucks on the chip. Pause.)*

CHARLIE.   Can I go watch Grandpa breathe?

LEE.   Charlie, don't word things that way.

BESSIE.   Sure you can. *(Charlie exits to Marvin's room.)*

RUTH.   *(From Marvin's room.)* Look who it is, Marvin. It's Charlie. No, he's real. Here Charlie. Do this. *(Ruth gives Charlie her mirror. He starts the light bouncing on Marvin's wall.)*

LEE.   Bessie, I'm sorry about all this. You should have quiet and I'm — I'm sorry. But this is what the doctor has asked me to do. I'm at the end of my rope. *(Sees the check.)* You tore up my check?

BESSIE.   Lee, I'm glad you're here but we've been getting along fine by ourselves for a long time and not because we've wanted to. That was your choice. Please, I'm glad to see you. I'm very grateful, but we're doing okay. *(Pause.)*

LEE.   *(She looks out the window.)* Hank, I can see you!!

Scene 7

Late at night in the backyard. Hank is examining tools in an old toolbox. Bessie enters with a cup of coffee.

BESSIE.   Hank?... Hank is that you?

HANK.   Yeah.

BESSIE. What are you doing out here?

HANK. Nothing.

BESSIE. It's kind of late to be up doing nothing.

HANK. What are you doing?

BESSIE. I'm having some coffee. Can't you sleep?

HANK. I don't need much sleep.

BESSIE. Growing boys need their sleep.

HANK. I'm done growing.

BESSIE. Do you want a sip of my coffee then?

HANK. No.

BESSIE. You gave me a scare Hank. I'm not used to finding someone else back here.

HANK. You want me to go inside?

BESSIE. No. Unless.... Are you not supposed to be out here? Will your mom care?

HANK. She's asleep.

BESSIE. I don't see any harm in it. But don't tell your Aunt Ruth that I wander away from the house at night. It might make her nervous.

HANK. She's not my aunt.

BESSIE. Sure she is.

HANK. She's my great aunt. You're my aunt. Marvin's my grandfather. I got a whole new family.

BESSIE. I guess you do. Must seem kind of strange.

HANK. No stranger than anything else.

BESSIE. We're all glad you're here.

HANK. Yeah, we should do it again in another seventeen years. *(Pause.)*

BESSIE. Do you like Florida so far?

HANK. Haven't seen much.

BESSIE. Nights like this are nice. You used to be able to see just a patch of the Gulf right through there.

HANK. Where?

BESSIE. You can't anymore. They built that elementary school. I don't know where they thought the kids would come from. You can still smell the water though.

HANK. I can't.

BESSIE. You can't? Maybe I just remember smelling it.

(Pause.) Your mom and I haven't always gotten along. That's why I haven't been in touch so much.

HANK. Uh-huh.

BESSIE. You sure did a lot of hard work around here this afternoon.

HANK. I was bored.

BESSIE. I knew Dad's respirator shouldn't rattle like that.

HANK. You just had to get those monopoly hotels that were crammed in there loose.

BESSIE. I wish you could have really known your grandfather. He'd a liked having a boy around.

HANK. He was kind of jabbering at me when I was in there.

BESSIE. That's his way of talking to you.

HANK. Kind of gave me the creeps.

BESSIE. Well, he's been sick for a very long time.

HANK. Don't you ever wish he would just die?

BESSIE. Hank.... Don't ask that.

HANK. Why not?

BESSIE. It's rude.

HANK. I haven't made up my mind about getting tested yet.

BESSIE. Hopefully your mom will be a match.

HANK. Even if she isn't, I just ...

BESSIE. Is that what you were doing? Sitting out here thinking about it?

HANK. No.

BESSIE. Oh. What were you thinking about? *(Pause.)* You don't have to tell me, of course. *(Pause.)* What are you doing with the tools?

HANK. I'm just looking at them. I was going to put them back.

BESSIE. I didn't think you were stealing them, Hank. You can have them if you want.

HANK. Really?

BESSIE. Sure.

HANK. You're giving them to me?

BESSIE. Sure.

HANK.   You're just giving them to me?

BESSIE.   Sure, why not?

HANK.   These are really cool tools.

BESSIE.   Are they?

HANK.   Yeah, they're ancient.

BESSIE.   That used to be your grandfather's toolbox. I think he'd like you to have it.

HANK.   They won't let me keep these, though.

BESSIE.   Who won't?

HANK.   The hospital.

BESSIE.   Well, you won't be in there forever.

HANK.   When I go back they're moving me to a place for adults.

BESSIE.   Why?

HANK.   I turn eighteen in three weeks.

BESSIE.   Oh. Happy birthday.

HANK.   Thanks. If the fire hadn't spread up the street it wouldn't be such a big deal.

BESSIE.   Uh-huh.

HANK.   Or if melting plastic didn't give off noxious fumes. Now they want to be sure I'm not a threat.

BESSIE.   You're not a threat. I'm sure they'll see that. You're probably the best one there.

HANK.   There's this one dude on my floor held a razor blade under his tongue for five hours. Talked to the orderlies and ate and everything.

BESSIE.   Why on earth would he do that?

HANK.   He was trying to break my record.

BESSIE.   Hank. What do you want to be when you grow up?

HANK.   I am grown up.

BESSIE.   When I look at you I see a lost little boy.

HANK.   Then get your eyes checked. *(Pause.)* So Marvin liked to fix stuff?

BESSIE.   Maybe that's where you get it from. He used to make your mom so mad. He'd leave the radio lying in pieces. She liked to turn it up and dance wild around the house.

HANK.   Mom liked to dance?

BESSIE.   You bet.

HANK.   *(Taking photo from toolbox.)* Hey, who is this?

BESSIE.   Let me see. *(They look at photo together.)* That's your grandmother.

HANK.   Looks kind of like Mom.

BESSIE.   She takes after her. Your grandfather used to have this taped above his workbench.

HANK.   She's young.

BESSIE.   She was young. *(Of photo.)* Do you want this too?

HANK.   I don't care.

BESSIE.   Then I'll keep it.

HANK.   Did you know my dad?

BESSIE.   I met him once. Doesn't your mom talk about him?

HANK.   I know he had a motorcycle.

BESSIE.   Did he?

HANK.   Yeah.

BESSIE.   I know your mom was nuts about him.

HANK.   Did you meet him at the wedding?

BESSIE.   No. It was when I pretty much knew that I was going to be down here with Dad and Ruth for longer than I thought. So I went back home to sell off the rest of my stuff.

HANK.   They have you over for dinner or something?

BESSIE.   No. I just sort of stopped by. I was curious to see this guy who could take up absolutely all of your mother's time. It wasn't much of a visit. He was asleep on the couch. Lee didn't want to wake him up and she had just mopped the kitchen floor so we stood in the hallway and talked for a while. When I left he was still asleep.

HANK.   How'd he seem?

BESSIE.   He seemed nice enough.

HANK.   I don't think I'll get the test. What do you think about that?

BESSIE.   Can I ask why?

HANK.   No reason. *(Pause.)* Being outside here is different than being outside at the hospital.

BESSIE.   How?

HANK.   Seems bigger.

BESSIE.   Maybe your mom wouldn't want you out this late.

HANK.   Okay.

BESSIE.   Did Ruth thank you for fixing the garage door?

HANK.   Yeah.

BESSIE.   That was very nice of you.

HANK.   Nobody ever does anything to be nice. That's what my therapist says.

BESSIE.   He does?

HANK.   People don't just do things. They get something for it.

BESSIE.   He says that?

HANK.   Yeah.

BESSIE.   And you believe him?

HANK.   Yeah.

BESSIE.   Why have I spent the last twenty years of my life down here. Because I enjoyed it?   Because I got something out of it?

HANK.   Yeah, or you wouldn't do it.

BESSIE.   No, Hank, no. Sometimes I can barely ... no.

HANK.   First time I hear from you is when you need something.

BESSIE.   Hank —

HANK.   Maybe you did it because maybe you thought you'd never land a husband. Or maybe you just wanted to hide out. When you're not around, a nursing home will do it for the cash.

BESSIE.   Your mom wouldn't let them go to a home.

HANK.   Why not? She doesn't give a shit about anybody.

LEE.   *(Off.)* Hank! Hank!

HANK.   *(Of tools.)* Where do you want me to put these?

BESSIE.   They're yours.

HANK.   Okay. *(He starts to go.)*

BESSIE.   Hank. You're my nephew and I love you no matter what you've decided.

Pause.

HANK.   Okay. *(He exits. Bessie stands alone as the lights fade to black.)*

ACT TWO

Scene 1

A retirement home. Bessie and Lee wait in a consulting room. A bowl of candies sits on the table.

BESSIE.   What's the time?

LEE.   You just asked me.

BESSIE.   What is it?

LEE.   Four twelve. *(Pause.)* Are you tired?

BESSIE.   No. *(Slight pause.)* Why? Do I look tired?

LEE.   You look good.

BESSIE.   Then why did you ask me?

LEE.   We've been waiting. I thought maybe you were tired of waiting.

BESSIE.   I am tired of waiting.

LEE.   That's all I meant. *(Pause.)* Why? Do you feel tired?

BESSIE.   I feel fine.

LEE.   You look great.

BESSIE.   I feel good. *(The Retirement Home Director enters and joins Bessie and Lee.)*

DIRECTOR.   Let me try to explain it again.

LEE.   I understood what you were saying.

DIRECTOR.   Then for your sister's benefit.

BESSIE.   You're saying I couldn't afford to put Dad and Ruth in this nursing home even if I wanted to.

DIRECTOR.   That's not what I'm saying.

LEE.   It's not?

DIRECTOR.   No.

LEE.   What are you saying?

DIRECTOR.   Let me say this, what does it matter what I'm saying if you have no interest in this institution?

LEE.   I didn't say that.

DIRECTOR.　She did.

LEE.　She didn't mean it.

BESSIE.　I think I did.

LEE.　Where do you want them to end up, Bessie? At County? For recreation they push the wheelchairs into the hall and let you watch the medicine carts roll by. Here they have computer games. They have nerf basketball.

DIRECTOR.　We have a video library. Sing-alongs. Date nights.

BESSIE.　Who is Dad going to date?

DIRECTOR.　You'd be surprised. Women outnumber the men five to one.

LEE.　This is the best place we've seen.

BESSIE.　We can't afford it so why are we talking?

DIRECTOR.　I never said that.

BESSIE.　What did you say?

DIRECTOR.　Let me get something that might help. *(Exits.)*

LEE.　I know this is hard. There's no reason to be depressed about my test results because I know Charlie is bound to match. So none of this means anything anyway because you're going to be fine.

BESSIE.　I don't like you pressuring Hank.

LEE.　What I'd like to do is take a stick to him. *(Pause.)*

BESSIE.　I have to take Charlie to Dr. Wally's and still get to the pharmacy before it closes.

LEE.　I'll take Charlie. We've got time. You've got more energy than I do. The way you handle Daddy and Ruth. I wouldn't last a week.

BESSIE.　It's not hard.

LEE.　You've done amazing things, Bessie.

BESSIE.　I haven't done so much.

LEE.　You should be proud.

BESSIE.　I just did what anybody would do.

LEE.　I get my degree next quarter.

BESSIE.　You should be proud of that.

LEE.　I already had one freelance job doing hair for a TV commercial. It was just local but guess how much they paid for one day.

BESSIE. I don't feel like guessing.

LEE. Guess.

BESSIE. Three hundred dollars.

LEE. That's right. Three hundred dollars. Why did you guess that?

BESSIE. It just popped into my head.

LEE. Most people would have guessed lower.

BESSIE. Three hundred dollars is a lot of money.

LEE. It's a lot for one day. I feel like my life is finally starting.

BESSIE. Who would take care of them here?

LEE. Doctors. Did you see they have a pool? They have a mirror ball in the cafeteria for disco night. This is a nice place. It even smells nice. Do you want a candy?

BESSIE. No.

LEE. I should take them all. She's kept us waiting so long. Serve her right. I could give them to the boys.

BESSIE. Don't steal them. She'll notice they're gone.

LEE. She's not going to accuse us. She'd be too embarrassed. *(She dumps the candies into her purse.)*

BESSIE. Lee!

LEE. Relax or she'll think you took them.

BESSIE. Put them back.

LEE. I can't. They're all rolling around in my purse.

DIRECTOR. *(Reenters with Xeroxes.)* All right. *(Gives them Xeroxes.)* If you turn to page four, you'll see a chart of the various state and national financial-aid programs for this institution. Do you see that? Page four.

BESSIE. I have the low-impact aerobic schedule.

LEE. So do I.

DIRECTOR. Here. *(Takes Xeroxes and exits.)*

BESSIE. Is the woman at the front desk a nurse?

LEE. She was wearing white.

BESSIE. They do that so you'll think there are more nurses around than there are. Did you touch her hands?

LEE. Why would I touch her hands?

BESSIE. They're ice. She has no circulation. I can't believe they let her touch patients.

LEE. She's probably just a receptionist.

BESSIE. So she's a fake.

LEE. She's not a fake. She's a real receptionist dressed in white.

BESSIE. Dad would have never done this.

LEE. Well.

BESSIE. Do you remember how he cared for Mom?

LEE. I was little. Mom was just this vague presence in a shut room at the end of the hall.

BESSIE. I remember.

LEE. We're doing the mature thing. We're seeing what our options are.

BESSIE. Why can't you take Dad and Ruth?

LEE. The nuns would love that.

BESSIE. You could move down here. You could have the house.

LEE. I don't think so.

BESSIE. Why not?

LEE. I've got Hank to think about.

BESSIE. He's very unhappy there.

LEE. Of course he's unhappy there. If he were happy he wouldn't be there.

BESSIE. You could find a nice place for him here, Lee. You'd have the whole house. The sunshine. You could find work down here.

LEE. No.

BESSIE. Give me one good reason.

LEE. Just no.

BESSIE. Why?

LEE. Because I don't want to. *(Pause.)* I made this decision once already. When Daddy had his first stroke, I made this decision then. I wasn't going to waste my life.

BESSIE. You think I've wasted my life?

LEE. Of course not.

BESSIE. I can't imagine a better way to have spent my life.

LEE. Then we both made the right decision.

BESSIE. You are the most ...

LEE. Say it. You've been saying it a million different ways

42

since I got down here.

BESSIE. I have not. I have bent over backwards to avoid having this conversation with you.

LEE. What conversation? *(Pause. Bessie opens her purse and puts about a dollar in change in the candy bowl.)* What are you doing?

BESSIE. I'm paying her for them.

LEE. Put that back.

BESSIE. I'm not going to steal them. It's wrong.

LEE. It's not wrong.

BESSIE. Wrong is wrong.

LEE. It's your money.

DIRECTOR. *(Reenters with Xeroxes.)* Turn to page four. You'll see a chart of the various financial-aid programs available.

LEE and BESSIE. *(Together.)* Uh-huh.

DIRECTOR. And you'll see that you don't qualify for any of them.

BESSIE. So you're wasting our time.

DIRECTOR. No. It means you have to drop into a lower income bracket.

BESSIE. Lower?

DIRECTOR. You need to deplete your savings on non-asset acquisitions. Including your home equity.

BESSIE. Lower?

DIRECTOR. Let me explain it again.

LEE. I understand.

DIRECTOR. Then for your sister's benefit. You need to spend your savings and your home equity on something that has no resale value and cannot be considered an asset. Seventy percent of our residents have done this to qualify for assistance.

LEE. What do they buy?

DIRECTOR. Most buy very elaborate tombstones. It's the perfect financial solution. *(Pause.)*

BESSIE. I'm going to wait in the car. *(She exits. Pause.)*

LEE. Do you have something I could take with me? *(The Director reaches to pick up a brochure off the table, sees the money in the candy bowl and looks at Lee.)*

Scene 2

The doctor's waiting room. Hank and Charlie sit in chairs near each other. Dr. Wally faces them. Bob stands by.

DR. WALLY.   Is everyone clear on the procedure we are about to do? Are there any questions?

BOB.   How long does the anesthetic take to work?

DR. WALLY.   It's not so important that you understand the procedure, Bob.

BOB.   *(To Hank and Charlie.)* Could I have your medical history cards, please? *(Hank and Charlie give them to him.)*

DR. WALLY.   Who is going to be the brave one and go first?

CHARLIE.   I want to go first. Can I?

HANK.   I don't care. *(Dr. Wally and Charlie start out.)*

DR. WALLY.   What grade are you in now, Hank?

CHARLIE.   I'm Charlie.

DR. WALLY.   I'm Dr. Wally. *(They exit.)*

BOB.   Hank, am I reading your medical card correctly? Are you currently on lithium?

HANK.   Yeah.

BOB.   It's a great drug, isn't it?

HANK.   Uh ...

BOB.   Can I ask you something? Did you find you put on a lot of weight since?

HANK.   No.

BOB.   No? Hmmm. *(He exits.)*

BESSIE.   *(Enters.)* Hank. I thought you'd be at home.

HANK.   No, I'm here.

BESSIE.   Where's your mom?

HANK.   She went over to the mall.

BESSIE.   Where's Charlie?

HANK.   He's in back already.

BESSIE.   Are you here to be with Charlie?

HANK.   I'll probably get tested too.

44

BESSIE. Nervous?

HANK. No.

BESSIE. These are new offices for them. Their old one became infested with bugs.

HANK. Bugs don't bother me.

BESSIE. No?

HANK. They crawl out of the drain in the boys' shower. They hide in the lumber in the wood shop. They float in the soap basins on the sinks. You get used to them.

BESSIE. I wouldn't.

HANK. One dude in my room. There's twelve of us in this room and this one dude catches bugs and puts them on a leash.

BESSIE. A leash?

HANK. A hair leash. He pulls out a strand of his hair and ties it around the bug and the other end he tacks down under his bunk. He had this whole zoo of bugs walking in little circles under his bed.

BESSIE. Hank.

HANK. Till this other dude smashed them all with the back of this cafeteria tray. It was funny.

BESSIE. Sounds funny.

HANK. It's not like anybody ate off the tray. It was an old tray. We use it to slide down the mud hill behind the seizure ward.

BESSIE. Uh-huh.

HANK. You get going real fast. This one dude's old man used to clock pitches for the National League East. He clocked me with his radar gun going fifty.

BESSIE. That's fast.

HANK. And my tray shot out from underneath me and broke this dude's windpipe. We had to perform an emergency tracheotomy with a sharp piece of bark and a Bic pen.

BESSIE. Hmmm.

HANK. Man, it was something. You want a candy? (*Offers her a candy from the retirement home.*)

BESSIE. No. Why do you make up these stories?

HANK. What?

BESSIE. These stories. Razors under the tongue, tracheotomies.

HANK. I'm not making anything up.

BESSIE. Why did you pretend you weren't going to get tested? Why did you put me through that?

HANK. I could still walk out of here.

BESSIE. Why do you tell so many lies?

HANK. I haven't told you shit. You don't know anything about that place.

BESSIE. Then tell me.

HANK. You don't know.

BESSIE. Tell me. *(Long pause.)*

HANK. You don't know.

BESSIE. I was in the hospital. It was boring. I was scared and it was boring.

HANK. There's this one dude —

BESSIE. If this is another tall tale I'm not interested. *(She picks up a magazine.)*

HANK. *(Sits.)* Toss me one, okay? *(Bessie gives him a magazine. They flip through them. Looking at a picture.)* Man, what magazine is this? *(He checks the cover and returns to picture.)* That's a human heart. *(Bessie pays him no attention.)* That's a kidney. That's a lung. That's a brain. That's the eye. That's skin. *(Pause.)* I played in a pool tournament in my ward. Did Mom tell you?

BESSIE. No.

HANK. I came in fourth. It's true. She doesn't think it's a big deal.

BESSIE. That's great. *(Slight pause.)*

HANK. I got my toe broken in there.

BESSIE. How?

HANK. Guy threw a garbage can at me and it landed on my foot.

BESSIE. Why'd he do that?

HANK. No reason I know of. Broken toes never heal.

BESSIE. Does it hurt?

HANK. Sometimes. *(Slight pause.)* A lot of drugs float around in there.

BESSIE.   Do you take them?

HANK.   Most of the time I keep to myself. Most of the time I sit in my room. I've got a roommate but most of the time he's got his face to the wall. Most of the time I think about not being there. I think what would it be like to be someone else. Someone I see on the TV or in a magazine, or even walking free on the grounds. They can keep me as long as they want. It's not like a prison term. I've already been there longer than most. A lot of the time I think about getting this house with all this land around it. And I'd get a bunch of dogs, no little ones you might step on but big dogs, like a horse, and I'd let them run wild. They'd never know a leash. And I'd build a go-cart track on my property. Charge people to race around on it. Those places pull in the bucks. I'd be raking it in. And nobody would know where I was. I'd be gone. Most of the time I just want to be someplace else.

BESSIE.   Why aren't you?

HANK.   Huh?

BESSIE.   Why aren't you someplace else?

HANK.   What do you mean?

BESSIE.   Do you want to be in there?

HANK.   No way.

BESSIE.   Then why are you?

HANK.   I've got no choice.

BESSIE.   You're the one who told me people only do what they want.

HANK.   Yeah.

BESSIE.   So you must want to be there.

HANK.   No. No way.

BESSIE.   Then show them you don't need to be in there.

HANK.   It's not easy like that. People start thinking of you a certain way and pretty soon you're that way.

BESSIE.   So there's nothing you can do?

HANK.   It's hard, that's all.

BESSIE.   I don't want you wasting your life in there.

HANK.   Neither do I.

BESSIE.   Then why are you still there?

HANK.   They put me there.

BESSIE.   Why'd they put you there?

HANK.   'Cause I burned down the house.

BESSIE.   Why'd you burn down the house? *(Slight pause.)*

DR. WALLY.   *(Enters.)* Hank, do you want to come on back? We can get you started while we're waiting for the anesthetic to start working on little Sammy.

HANK.   Charlie.

DR. WALLY.   I'm sorry. Did I call you Hank? It's these new offices. Do you want to come back? *(Exits.)*

HANK.   Would you come back with me?

BESSIE.   Sure I would. *(They exit.)*

Scene 3

Bessie's home. Night. Charlie and Hank on the floor in sleeping bags.

CHARLIE.   *(After a moment, sits up.)* Hank?

HANK.   Yeah.

CHARLIE.   Do you ever think about actually dying? *(Pause.)*

HANK.   No. Do you?

CHARLIE.   No. *(Pause.)* Hank, what do you want for your birthday?

HANK.   I don't care.

CHARLIE.   I wish we never had to go home. *(He pulls the sleeping bag up over his head.)*

HANK.   Can you breathe like that?

CHARLIE.   Yeah. *(Pause.)* Hank?

HANK.   Yeah.

CHARLIE.   Are you excited about Walt Disney World? *(Pause.)*

HANK.   Yeah. Are you?

CHARLIE.   Yeah. *(Lights fade on Charlie and Hank as Bessie enters kitchen area. Bessie pours herself coffee. The only light we see is from the refrigerator when she opens the door to get out the cream. After a while, Lee enters in the dark. She turns on the light. Bessie*

*is standing there without her wig, frozen for a moment, like a rab-
bit caught in the headlights.)*

LEE.   Oh.

BESSIE.   I was just going to bed. *(Exits. Lee pours juice and
vodka. Reenters wearing wig.)* Forgot my coffee.

LEE.   Why are you drinking coffee so late?

BESSIE.   I like it. Why are you up?

LEE.   I guess I was thirsty.

BESSIE.   Did you find everything you need?

LEE.   Yes. Thank you.

BESSIE.   You're welcome. The boys didn't eat much at dinner.

LEE.   No. You have a way with Hank.

BESSIE.   I don't.

LEE.   You do. You have a way with him.

BESSIE.   He's a good boy.

LEE.   Is he?

BESSIE.   Sure he is.

LEE.   I wish I knew your secret.

BESSIE.   I just talk to him.

LEE.   Are you saying I don't? *(Slight pause.)*

BESSIE.   *(Starts to exit.)* I'm tired and we've got Disney World
tomorrow.

LEE.   You know, I could fix your wig for you.

BESSIE.   Fix it?

LEE.   I could style it for you. I know how.

BESSIE.   Does it look bad?

LEE.   No, but if you've got a wig you should have fun with
it. Try different looks.

BESSIE.   Uh-huh.

LEE.   Something sporty or a sophisticated out-on-the-town
evening thing.

BESSIE.   I just brush it out now and then.

LEE.   I've got a whole makeup kit down here too.

BESSIE.   I don't bother with that much.

LEE.   You should. I mean because it's fun. And you never
know when you might meet someone.

BESSIE.   Meet someone?

LEE.   Sure.

BESSIE.   A man?

LEE.   Yes, a man.

BESSIE.   I haven't thought about a man in years.

LEE.   You're lying.

BESSIE.   I'm sorry we haven't been seeing eye to eye.

LEE.   When?

BESSIE.   At the nursing home.

LEE.   I don't remember anything about it.

BESSIE.   I don't want us to fight.

LEE.   I don't think we have been.

BESSIE.   I want us to get along.

LEE.   We do get along.

BESSIE.   I don't want us to just get along. I don't want us to be polite.

LEE.   I've never had a problem with that.

BESSIE.   I want us to ... I want ... *(Pause.)* Not much seems important to me now.

LEE.   We're sisters.

BESSIE.   The past is —

LEE.   We're sisters.

BESSIE.   I want you to know —

LEE.   I do know. *(Marvin stirs in his room.)* Should we?

BESSIE.   Just sit quiet for a moment. He scares himself sometimes. He'll go back to sleep. *(They're quiet.)*

LEE.   Do you remember when Daddy used to drive us down to Miami for vacations?

BESSIE.   Sure I do. The two of us asleep in the back seat.

LEE.   How'd we fit?

BESSIE.   Tuna sandwiches sliding across the dash.

LEE.   Daddy had the talk radio on real low.

BESSIE.   It'd be so cold outside.

LEE.   The gasman would run out from his warm office and pump our gas without bothering with a coat. Waitresses would lift me light as a feather over someone's head and plop me down in the back of a booth. Everyone seemed so strong to me then.

BESSIE.   We were little.

LEE.   Seemed like such a long trip.

BESSIE.   Forever. *(Marvin stirs again. They are quiet a moment.)* Are you seeing anybody now?

LEE.   Usually.

BESSIE.   I hope you have someone real in your life.

LEE.   I don't have much trouble with that.

BESSIE.   I'm not talking about "that."

LEE.   You should be. There's no reason you haven't had love in your life.

BESSIE.   I think I've —

LEE.   Men. There's no reason. You're not ugly, Bessie.

BESSIE.   Thank you.

LEE.   You're not. I know lots of boys were interested in you, they just thought you were stuck up.

BESSIE.   Thank you.

LEE.   Well, if you had given them any encouragement.

BESSIE.   I had a true love.

LEE.   You did?

BESSIE.   Yes.

LEE.   Did he know?

BESSIE.   Yes.

LEE.   You mean you had a boyfriend?

BESSIE.   Yes, I had a boyfriend. Why is that such news?

LEE.   How could I not have known about it?

BESSIE.   It wasn't anyone you knew.

LEE.   Bart Martick.

BESSIE.   No. Why do you say Bart Martick?

LEE.   I remember you used to stare at him out of the side of your face.

BESSIE.   No, I don't remember that. Well, maybe I would stare at him because he had that lazy eye but it was never anything romantic.

LEE.   Who then?

BESSIE.   You don't know him.

LEE.   You can tell me Bessie. It's not like I'm going to tell anybody.

BESSIE.   Clarence James.

LEE.   Who?

BESSIE.   I told you you didn't know him.

LEE.   How could I not know him?

BESSIE.   He was only around in the summers. *(Pause.)*

LEE.   *(Catching on.)* You went with a carny worker.

BESSIE.   He was a very nice person.

LEE.   I didn't say anything.

BESSIE.   This is why I kept it a secret.

LEE.   I didn't say anything. Daddy would have killed you.

BESSIE.   Well he's never going to know.

LEE.   There were some cute ones.

BESSIE.   He was cute.

LEE.   Which one was he?

BESSIE.   He mostly ran the ferris wheel.

LEE.   Uh-huh.

BESSIE.   I knew he liked me because he always gave me an extra turn.

LEE.   That's sweet.

BESSIE.   Once he kept my car swaying at the top until I started to cry.

LEE.   He was a flirt.

BESSIE.   He had these big ears.

LEE.   I remember him. He was cute.

BESSIE.   He always said he probably came from England because of his name. Clarence James. He'd make a big deal out of his manners. He had the funniest laugh. He'd open his mouth real wide and no sound would come out.

LEE.   He was only there about three summers.

BESSIE.   Four summers.

LEE.   Then he stopped coming.

BESSIE.   That's right. *(Pause.)*

LEE.   What happened?

BESSIE.   Nothing like you think.

LEE.   What happened?

BESSIE.   They always have a last picnic down by the river. This year there was kind of a cold snap so a lot of people were bundled up. But Clarence, he'll deny it, but he likes to be the center of attention. Clarence goes swimming anyway. And he knows everybody is watching him. Everybody is there, his family, his friends, me. And he bobs up out of the water and he's laughing, making that monkey face, which gets all of us laughing, and he dunks under again and pops up somewhere else laughing even harder which gets us laughing even harder. And he dives under again and then he doesn't come up and he doesn't come up and he doesn't come up. Laughing and choking looked the same on Clarence. He drowned right in front of us. Every time he came up for air, there we were chuckling and pointing. What could he have thought?

LEE. Bessie, you should have told me.

BESSIE. If I couldn't tell people I had a carny boyfriend, I couldn't tell people my carny boyfriend drowned.

LEE. You should have told me anyway.

BESSIE. We were never that close.

LEE. Weren't we?

BESSIE. No. *(Pause.)*

LEE. Do you want me to do something with that wig?

BESSIE. What?

LEE. I don't know. Let me look at it. *(Bessie turns her head, giving her a look.)* No, you have to take it off.

BESSIE. Oh.

LEE. I won't hurt it. *(Bessie is reluctant to give Lee the wig.)* This is a nice wig, Bessie. It's nicely ventilated. We can do something with this. Do you want me to?

BESSIE. Sure. *(Bessie takes off her wig and hands it to Lee. A long pause as Lee takes in the effects of Bessie's chemotherapy.)*

LEE. I'm glad we made this trip. I only wish we could stay longer. This is a nice weave.

RUTH. *(Enters.)* Bessie? Bessie?

BESSIE. Ruth? *(She ties a scarf over her head.)*

RUTH. I went by your room. You weren't there.

BESSIE. I'm here.

RUTH. It was empty.

BESSIE. I'm here. *(Ruth hugs Bessie hard.)* Oh, honey, I'm still here. Honeybunch. *(Lee stands and watches Bessie and Ruth embraced.)*

Scene 4

Walt Disney World. Hank sits alone on a bench. Lee enters with two Cokes. She gives one to Hank and joins him on the bench. They drink.

LEE. These are expensive.

HANK. This is the Diet.

LEE. Is it? *(They switch drinks. They drink.)* That Swiss Family Robinson tree house is huge.

HANK. I guess.

LEE. We saw that movie. Do you remember? I took you. I took you both. That's when I was still driving the Plymouth. Do you remember?

HANK. I don't remember.

LEE. I took you both to that movie.

HANK. I remember Dad took us to *The Planet of the Apes.*

LEE. No, he didn't.

HANK. He didn't?

LEE. I took you to that but you were older then. *(Pause.)*

HANK. That was a good movie.

LEE. The one with the apes?

HANK. Uh-huh.

LEE. Oh good. I'm glad you liked it. Are you having a good time?

HANK. Where's Charlie?

LEE. They're probably still at the Hall of Presidents. You didn't want to see that. I'm proud of you Hank, getting tested for Bessie.

HANK. Are we going to sit here all day?

LEE. We're supposed to meet them here. Maybe we'll eat. Or we'll see that movie that wraps around you.

HANK. Charlie and I want to go to Space Mountain.

LEE. We'll do that.

HANK. We want to go off by ourselves.

LEE. No. Uh-uh. I've already gone back on my ultimatum

just letting you come. I think you're doing really well this trip. I think everyone is going to hear how well you did. I think it will mean a lot to them. For the most part your behavior down here has made me very happy, but no. *(Pause.)* That submarine ride. Now, that's a movie too.

HANK.   Did we see that one?

LEE.   Did you? *(She tries hard to remember.)* I don't think so. I don't remember.

HANK.   With Dad?

LEE.   No, no, no, not with your dad. Do you like apes? Do you like animals? *(Hank stands and hurls his Coke offstage. He sits.)* Hank! You're not getting another one. *(Pause.)* Do you want to know something about your dad? On Saturday I worked and your dad took care of you.

HANK.   He did?

LEE.   Yeah. And sometimes on Saturdays you'd get hurt. And I know you roughhoused too much. And I'd yell at you for roughhousing too much, but you'd still get hurt. And I started leaving my job early so I could get home, and.... I'd yell at you and yell at you and beg you to please stop hurting yourself because he was my husband, and I loved him and what was I supposed to do? Then Charlie came and I just ... *(Pause.)* My feelings for you, Hank, are like a big bowl of fish-hooks. I can't just pick them up one at a time. I pick up one, they all come. So I tend to leave them alone. *(Charlie pushes Ruth on in a wheelchair. Charlie is wearing a "Goofy" cap and Ruth a sun hat.)*

RUTH.   Oh! There you are. It's like a piece of heaven fell from the sky. Isn't it? So many handsome young men and women. Everyone is so nice. Mickey Mouse pushed my chair for a little while. Didn't he Charlie?

CHARLIE.   He did.

LEE.   Is he still 'round? I want to get a picture.

RUTH.   I don't know where he went. He's probably very busy.

LEE.   Where's Bessie?

RUTH.   She's getting Cokes for everyone.

LEE.   She is?

55

RUTH.   You should have come with us. You don't know what you missed.

LEE.   Did you like the Hall of Presidents?

RUTH.   It was so nice to see F.D.R. again.

LEE.   Are you hungry, Charlie?

CHARLIE.   *(Has started reading a book.)* Not yet.

LEE.   Charlie, please don't read. You're at Disney World. Look around.

RUTH.   Do you want me to hold your book on my lap?

CHARLIE.   No.

LEE.   Read your book if you want. It doesn't matter. *(Bessie enters with a tray of Cokes. Her wig has been styled. It looks very nice.)*

BESSIE.   Here we are. I hope everyone is thirsty. Hank. *(She gives him a Coke.)* Lee.

LEE.   I already have one.

BESSIE.   We have an extra then. Hank you look extra thirsty. *(She gives him a second one.)* Ruth.

RUTH.   It looks nice and cold.

BESSIE.   Charlie. Isn't it a beautiful day? I feel like I haven't been outside in years.

LEE.   Did you like the Hall of Presidents?

BESSIE.   It was kind of fun to see J.F.K. again.

RUTH.   *(Starts waving frantically.)* Lee, there's one of those cartoon characters if you want to get a picture.

LEE.   Who is that? Pluto?

RUTH.   It looks more like a gopher than a dog.

BESSIE.   Those aren't gopher ears.

LEE.   Is Pluto a dog?

CHARLIE.   *(Looks up from his book.)* Yes.

BESSIE.   They look like horse ears.

LEE.   Let's get our picture taken with it.

HANK.   I don't want my picture taken with some mutant.

BESSIE.   Should we wait for someone more Disney?

RUTH.   Like Daisy Duck?

LEE.   C'mon Hank.

BESSIE.   This you can probably see at Six Flags.

LEE.   But we're all together now. I'm going to ask him to

come over. *(She exits.)*

HANK.   Charlie, let's go to Space Mountain.

CHARLIE.   Okay.

BESSIE.   I don't think your mom wants you to go off alone.

HANK.   She doesn't care.

BESSIE.   I think she does.

HANK.   We'll be right back.

BESSIE.   Hank, stay here.

HANK.   We'll only be gone a second.

BESSIE.   Hank, please.

HANK.   Okay.

LEE.   *(Reenters.)* That was the rudest cartoon character I've ever met. He knew damn well what I was asking him, but he just kept bobbing his head and waving his hooves at me like some dumb animal.

RUTH.   Hooves?

LEE.   Hooves, paws. Was I supposed to tip him?

CHARLIE.   No.

LEE.   Well, we'll just have to get someone else. What did you want to do next Ruth? See "It's a Small World?"

RUTH.   If everyone else does.

LEE.   Sure, why don't we?

BESSIE.   You all go ahead. I want to sit here a bit.

LEE.   We can sit longer.

BESSIE.   No. I'm fine. I just want to sit in the sun. I'll catch up to you.

LEE.   Where?

HANK.   How about Space Mountain?

BESSIE.   Space Mountain in an hour?

LEE.   Okay.

RUTH.   Why don't you come Bessie?

BESSIE.   It feels good to sit in the sun. And if I come somebody will have to ride by themselves.

LEE.   We'll see you in front of Space Mountain in an hour. Right where the line starts.

BESSIE.   I'll be there.

LEE.   Charlie, do you want me to push your aunt for a while?

CHARLIE.   I like pushing.
RUTH.   You're a good driver. *(They are off. Bessie shuts her eyes and breathes deeply. She is not feeling well. The feeling passes. She sips her Coke through a straw. The straw comes away bloody. She puts her finger in her mouth. More blood. She stares at it. She puts her hand to her mouth. There is blood in her mouth. It gets on her hand. She stands as if to leave. A Cartoon Character enters as Bessie faints and falls to the ground. The Cartoon Character turns and walks toward the audience, waving as the lights fade.)*

Scene 5

Walt Disney World. The Lost Children's hut. Bessie lies on a small bed. Lee sits in a small chair. Bessie wakes up violently as if from a nightmare.

LEE.   You're all right.
BESSIE.   Hmmmm.
LEE.   You're all right.
BESSIE.   Where am I?
LEE.   You're in the Lost Children's hut.
BESSIE.   Where?
RUTH.   *(Appears in the doorway.)* Bessie?
LEE.   She's okay, Ruth.
BESSIE.   Ruth?
RUTH.   Bessie?
BESSIE.   I'm fine.
RUTH.   Are you all right now?
BESSIE.   I just got real tired.
RUTH.   You should rest.
BESSIE.   I am.
RUTH.   You do too much. You always do too much.
BESSIE.   I won't do so much anymore. I promise.
LEE.   She's fine Ruth.
BESSIE.   We've only paid Dad's nurse till seven o'clock.
LEE.   Don't worry about that.

BESSIE. Is there a phone?

RUTH. I'll call. *(She exits.)*

LEE. Dr. Serat and Dr. Wally are meeting us at the hospital.

BESSIE. Dr. Serat?

LEE. He's back.

BESSIE. I have to go back in the hospital?

LEE. They want to look at you. If you feel good there's no reason you can't come home.

BESSIE. I feel good.

LEE. What happened?

BESSIE. I fainted.

LEE. From the heat?

BESSIE. There was blood in my mouth.

LEE. Is your mouth still bleeding?

BESSIE. No. Did a doctor look at me?

LEE. No. He just thought you fainted so he carried you in here to lie down.

BESSIE. Who's he?

LEE. The gopher man.

BESSIE. The gopher man?

LEE. Yes.

BESSIE. Carried me to the Lost Children's hut?

LEE. He just thought you fainted. He didn't know you had been bleeding.

BESSIE. I couldn't have bled that much.

LEE. Maybe you were kind of faint from not eating, too. That might be all it is.

BESSIE. I fainted because ... I was scared.

LEE. You're all right.

BESSIE. I was so scared.

LEE. That's okay.

BESSIE. What's happening to me?

LEE. Shhh.

BESSIE. I can't sleep anymore. I never sleep. I'm afraid to close my eyes. I'll close my eyes and I won't wake up. So I jerk myself awake. I yank myself awake all night long.

LEE. Bessie ...

BESSIE. I pour myself some coffee.

LEE. It's okay.

BESSIE. I just want to find a place to hide.

LEE. You're okay.

BESSIE. I'm trying to be brave.

LEE. Shh. Shh.

BESSIE. But I'm scared. I'm so scared. *(They hug.)*

LEE. Shh. Shh. You're okay. Oh, you're okay. *(Comforts her silently.)* What have you got to be scared of? Everything is going to be okay. You'll see. There's still Hank and Charlie. Are you forgetting that? You're okay.

BESSIE. Where are they?

LEE. They're sitting out front.

BESSIE. Was Space Mountain fun?

LEE. Uh-huh, it was real fun.

BESSIE. You're lucky to have those boys.

LEE. I know I am.

BESSIE. They're good boys, both of them.

LEE. Yes, they are.

BESSIE. And you know?

LEE. What?

BESSIE. I'm lucky to have Dad and Ruth.

LEE. Mm-hmm.

BESSIE. I've had such love in my life. I look back and I've had such love.

LEE. They love you very much.

BESSIE. I don't mean — I mean I love them. I am so lucky to have been able to love someone so much. I am so lucky to have loved so much. I am so lucky.

LEE. Yes, you are. You are.

BESSIE. We're fooling ourselves, Lee. *(Hank appears in the doorway.)*

LEE. How?

BESSIE. Hank and Charlie aren't going to match.

LEE. We don't know that.

BESSIE. They're my nephews. They're once removed.

LEE. It could still happen.

BESSIE. I don't want to pretend any longer. We have too

60

many decisions to make before you leave.

LEE.   We don't have to make them right now.

HANK.   Is that true?

LEE.   *(Notices Hank.)* Hank, would you find me a wheelchair.

HANK.   Charlie is.

LEE.   Do you feel up to going to the car?

BESSIE.   Oh, sure. *(Bessie sits up. Charlie enters with a wheelchair and stops it next to the tiny chair. Hank picks Bessie up and puts her in the wheelchair. She looks at the tiny chair.)* I don't remember ever being that small.

LEE.   Ready?

Scene 6

Night. Hank and Charlie in their sleeping bags.

HANK.   Charlie? Charlie? *(Pause. He goes to Charlie, straddles him and shines a penlight in his face.)* Charlie?

CHARLIE.   What?

HANK.   What are you doing?

CHARLIE.   Sleeping. What are you doing?

HANK.   Can't sleep.

CHARLIE.   How come?

HANK.   How come you do so bad in school?

CHARLIE.   I don't know.

HANK.   You gotta study more.

CHARLIE.   Get off me.

HANK.   This is cool. Your eyes shrink when I shine the light on them.

CHARLIE.   I can't breathe.

HANK.   And quit letting Mom buy all your clothes. You look like a geek.

CHARLIE.   You're going to make me blind.

HANK.   And pay more attention. Okay?

CHARLIE.   Okay. *(Hank sits back down. Pause.)* I don't think I look so bad.

HANK. Did you hear what I said?

CHARLIE. Yeah.

HANK. Okay. Charlie, how much money you got down here?

CHARLIE. I have fifteen dollars and thirty-six cents left.

HANK. Why'd you buy that stupid Goofy cap?

CHARLIE. I like it.

HANK. If I ever take anything from you, you know I'll find a way to pay you back. *(Pause.)*

CHARLIE. Hank?

HANK. Go to sleep now.

Scene 7

Bessie's home. Ruth sits in her chair. Charlie stands over her. Lee's makeup kit is open and spread on Ruth's lap. Ruth is dressed up.

RUTH. Try this one. *(Hands him an eyeliner.)*

CHARLIE. I'm afraid I'll poke you in the eye.

RUTH. Oh, no. I trust you. You've got a steady hand. Not like me.

CHARLIE. Look up. *(Applies eyeliner.)*

RUTH. Not too heavy.

CHARLIE. Okay.

RUTH. I don't mean to tell you what to do.

CHARLIE. No, tell me.

RUTH. I haven't had reason to pretty myself up since, I can't think when.

CHARLIE. Today's the day.

RUTH. I hope nothing goes wrong. They almost got married once before but the church caught fire.

CHARLIE. Is Coral the same character who shot Lance's dad in the head?

RUTH. Mm-hm.

CHARLIE. And now they're getting married?

RUTH.   Well, he lived. And she felt awful about it.

CHARLIE.   How's that?

RUTH.   Oh, what a good job.

CHARLIE.   You look pretty.

RUTH.   I do not. If I look anything at all it's because you're such a help. Charlie, where's Hank? I want him to move the TV from my room into Bessie's room so she can watch too.

CHARLIE.   I can do it.

RUTH.   Are you sure?

CHARLIE.   Yeah.

RUTH.   *(As he goes.)* It's awfully heavy. *(Charlie exits.)*

LEE.   *(Enters.)* Let me see, Ruth. Oh, you're beautiful.

RUTH.   Don't make fun of me.

LEE.   I'm not.

RUTH.   I'm a silly old woman dressing up for a TV show.

LEE.   You're not. I'm going to make some snacks so we won't be getting up during the program.

RUTH.   Oh, my. It's becoming such a production. Is everybody going to watch?

LEE.   I don't know if Hank is. I don't know where he's got to.

RUTH.   I'll find him.

LEE.   It's so nice to have you up and around, Ruth. It must be wonderful to be rid of constant pain.

RUTH.   Oh, yes. Though I do sometimes miss it. *(Exits. Lee puts chips in a bowl. Charlie reenters reading his book, takes some chips, crosses to chair and begins to read. Bessie enters.)*

LEE.   What are you doing up?

BESSIE.   I'm going to give Dad his one o'clock.

LEE.   I was going to do that.

BESSIE.   Oh, I can do it.

LEE.   You're supposed to be taking it easy.

BESSIE.   I am.

LEE.   Do you want something to snack on?

BESSIE.   Better just cut me up some fruit. *(Phone rings.)*

LEE.   *(Answers.)* Hello? Hello Dr. Serat.

BESSIE.   What is it?

LEE.   It's Dr. Serat. He wants to talk to you.

BESSIE. *(Taking phone.)* Hello. Oh, you did. Good. Um ... uh, what is — . I see. I see. Uh-huh. Then should I keep taking what I'm taking now? No, I understand. I'm not. Thank you doctor. Goodbye. *(Hangs up.)* They got Hank and Charlie's test results back and it looks like it didn't work out.

LEE. Oh, Bessie.

BESSIE. That's pretty much what we expected. We knew the odds were against it.

LEE. Maybe we should do them again. Maybe they made a mistake.

BESSIE. Maybe but I don't.... I'm supposed to continue with the therapies I'm doing now and see what kind of luck I have.

LEE. That's right. Those are good things to be doing.

BESSIE. Where's Hank? We should tell Hank. I was in the middle of doing something. What was I...? Oh, Dad. *(She reaches for the pills and knocks them onto the floor. The pills spill all over.)*

LEE. Do you want to go lie down?

BESSIE. No. I'm fine, I just ... *(She starts picking up the pills.)*

LEE. I can do that. Charlie. *(Charlie and Lee help pick up pills.)*

BESSIE. It's what we thought. It's not a surprise. It's what I always had in the back of my head. Now I don't have to think about it anymore. I can quit thinking about it. *(Sigh of relief.)* Oh, I can quit thinking about it. We should tell Hank.

LEE. Charlie, where's your brother?

CHARLIE. He's gotta be somewhere.

LEE. Hank? *(Exits.)*

CHARLIE. Hank ran away.

BESSIE. What?

CHARLIE. He ran away last night.

BESSIE. Oh, Charlie, no.

CHARLIE. He left you this. *(He hands her a note. Bessie reads note to herself.)* I didn't read it.

BESSIE. *(Reads note to Charlie.)* "Aunt Bessie, gone someplace else. Goodbye, good luck. I love you, too. Hank."

CHARLIE. He said he was sorry he couldn't wait. *(They hug.)*

BESSIE.   Oh Charlie. We have to tell your mother.

CHARLIE.   I promised I wouldn't tell until tonight.

BESSIE.   Charlie, she has to know.

CHARLIE.   Aunt Bessie, I promised. It was the last thing I said.

BESSIE.   Do you want me to tell her?

CHARLIE.   I promised.

BESSIE.   Why don't you go on outside? *(Charlie exits. Bessie reads the note again. She is overcome and begins to break down when Marvin stirs in his room.)* Dad? What is it? What's wrong. It's just me. There's nothing to be afraid of. *(Marvin calms down.)* There's nothing to be afraid of. *(She leaves the note on the counter and goes into Marvin's room. Lee enters and sees pills on floor. She picks up the pill bottle. She crosses to the counter to put the pills down. She sees Hank's note and reads it to herself. After a few moments she crumples the note, tosses it on the counter and begins to exit. Before she can leave, Hank enters with his bags. He does not see Lee. He crosses to the chair, drops his bags, goes to look into Marvin's room, stops, turns back to the chair and sees Lee. The two look at each other from across the room. Hank removes his bandana.)*

RUTH.   *(Off.)* Hurry up, Charlie. The show's starting. *(Hank crosses past Lee and exits off stage. Lee crosses to the chair and picks up Hank's bags.)*

BESSIE.   *(From Marvin's room.)* Here, let me do this for you. *(Bessie starts bouncing the light around Marvin's room. Lee exits. The lights fade except for one on Bessie and Marvin. Then the lights grow very bright in Marvin's room. After a moment, they fade back down except for the one on Bessie and Marvin, who are heard laughing. Then the lights fade completely out.)*

END OF PLAY

PROPERTY LIST

Syringe (DR. WALLY)
Tourniquet (DR. WALLY)
Vials (DR. WALLY)
Bag of cotton balls (DR. WALLY)
Magazines
Groceries (BESSIE)
Marvin's pills in vials (BESSIE)
Ruth's vitamins (RUTH)
Soup can (BESSIE)
Metal pan (BESSIE)
Compact mirror (RUTH)
Coffee in styrofoam cup (BOB)
Cigarette (LEE, DR. CHARLOTTE)
Lighter or matches (LEE, DR. CHARLOTTE)
Glass ashtray (DR. CHARLOTTE)
Lunch meal (BESSIE)
TV remote control
Sheets (BESSIE)
Checks and pen (LEE)
Book (CHARLIE)
Bowl of potato chips
Toolbox (HANK) with:
    tools
    photos
Cup of coffee (BESSIE)
Bowl of candies
Change (coins) (BESSIE)
Medical history card (CHARLIE, HANK)
Coffee pot (BESSIE)
Cup (BESSIE)
Cream for coffee (BESSIE)
Juice (LEE)

Vodka (LEE)
Glass (LEE)
2 Coca-Colas in cups (LEE)
Wheelchair (RUTH, CHARLIE)
"Goofy" cap (CHARLIE)
Sun hat (RUTH)
Tray with 5 Coca-Colas in cups (BESSIE)
Penlight (CHARLIE)
Makeup kit, full (LEE)

SOUND EFFECTS

Phone ring
Soap opera theme music
Doorbell
Garage door going up

NEW PLAYS

★ **CLOSER by Patrick Marber.** Winner of the 1998 Olivier Award for Best Play and the 1999 New York Drama Critics Circle Award for Best Foreign Play. Four lives intertwine over the course of four and a half years in this densely plotted, stinging look at modern love and betrayal. "CLOSER is a sad, savvy, often funny play that casts a steely, unblinking gaze at the world of relationships ... CLOSER does not merely hold your attention; it burrows into you." –*New York Magazine* "A powerful, darkly funny play about the cosmic collision between the sun of love and the comet of desire." –*Newsweek Magazine* [2M, 2W] ISBN: 0-8222-1722-8

★ **THE MOST FABULOUS STORY EVER TOLD by Paul Rudnick.** A stage manager, headset and prompt book at hand, brings the house lights to half, then dark, and cues the creation of the world. Throughout the play, she's in control of everything. In other words, she's either God, or she thinks she is. "Line by line, Mr. Rudnick may be the funniest writer for the stage in the United States today ... One-liners, epigrams, withering put-downs and flashing repartee: These are the candles that Mr. Rudnick lights instead of cursing the darkness ... a testament to the virtues of laughing ... and in laughter, there is something like the memory of Eden." –*The NY Times* "Funny it is ... consistently, rapaciously, deliriously ... easily the funniest play in town." –*Variety* [4M, 5W] ISBN: 0-8222-1720-1

★ **A DOLL'S HOUSE by Henrik Ibsen, adapted by Frank McGuinness.** Winner of the 1997 Tony Award for Best Revival. "New, raw, gut-twisting and gripping. Easily the hottest drama this season." –*USA Today* "Bold, brilliant and alive." –*The Wall Street Journal* "A thunderclap of an evening that takes your breath away." –*Time Magazine* [4M, 4W, 2 boys] ISBN: 0-8222-1636-1

★ **THE HERBAL BED by Peter Whelan.** The play is based on actual events which occurred in Stratford-upon-Avon in the summer of 1613, when William Shakespeare's elder daughter was publicly accused of having a sexual liaison with a married neighbor and family friend. "In his probing new play, THE HERBAL BED ... Peter Whelan muses about a sidelong event in the life of Shakespeare's family and creates a finely textured tapestry of love and lies in the early 17th-century Stratford." –*The NY Times* "It is a first rate drama with interesting moral issues of truth and expediency." –*The NY Post* [5M, 3W] ISBN: 0-8222-1675-2

★ **SNAKEBIT by David Marshall Grant.** A study of modern friendship when put to the test. "... a rather smart and absorbing evening of water-cooler theater, the intimate sort of Off-Broadway experience that has you picking apart the recognizable characters long after the curtain calls." – *The NY Times* "Off-Broadway keeps on presenting us with compelling reasons for going to the theater. The latest is SNAKEBIT, David Marshall Grant's smart new comic drama about being thirtysomething and losing one's way in life." –*The NY Daily News* [3M, 1W] ISBN: 0-8222-1724-4

★ **A QUESTION OF MERCY by David Rabe.** The Obie Award-winning playwright probes the sensitive and controversial issue of doctor-assisted suicide in the age of AIDS in this poignant drama. "There are many devastating ironies in Mr. Rabe's beautifully considered, piercingly clear-eyed work ..." –*The NY Times* "With unsettling candor and disturbing insight, the play arouses pity and understanding of a troubling subject ... Rabe's provocative tale is an affirmation of dignity that rings clear and true." –*Variety* [6M, 1W] ISBN: 0-8222-1643-4

★ **DIMLY PERCEIVED THREATS TO THE SYSTEM by Jon Klein.** Reality and fantasy overlap with hilarious results as this unforgettable family attempts to survive the nineties. "Here's a play whose point about fractured families goes to the heart, mind – and ears." –*The Washington Post* "... an end-of-the-millennium comedy about a family on the verge of a nervous breakdown ... Trenchant and hilarious ..." –*The Baltimore Sun* [2M, 4W] ISBN: 0-8222-1677-9

DRAMATISTS PLAY SERVICE, INC.
440 Park Avenue South, New York, NY 10016 212-683-8960 Fax 212-213-1539
postmaster@dramatists.com www.dramatists.com

NEW PLAYS

★ **AS BEES IN HONEY DROWN by Douglas Carter Beane.** Winner of the John Gassner Playwriting Award. A hot young novelist finds the subject of his new screenplay in a New York socialite who leads him into the world of *Auntie Mame* and *Breakfast at Tiffany's*, before she takes him for a ride. "A delicious soufflé of a satire ... [an] extremely entertaining fable for an age that always chooses image over substance." *–The NY Times* "... A witty assessment of one of the most active and relentless industries in a consumer society ... the creation of 'hot' young things, which the media have learned to mass produce with efficiency and zeal." *–The NY Daily News* [3M, 3W, flexible casting] ISBN: 0-8222-1651-5

★ **STUPID KIDS by John C. Russell.** In rapid, highly stylized scenes, the story follows four high-school students as they make their way from first through eighth period and beyond, struggling with the fears, frustrations, and longings peculiar to youth. "In STUPID KIDS ... playwright John C. Russell gets the opera of adolescence to a T ... The stylized teenspeak of STUPID KIDS ... suggests that Mr. Russell may have hidden a tape recorder under a desk in study hall somewhere and then scoured the tapes for good quotations ... it is the kids' insular, ceaselessly churning world, a pre-adult world of Doritos and libidos, that the playwright seeks to lay bare." *–The NY Times* "STUPID KIDS [is] a sharp-edged ... whoosh of teen angst and conformity anguish. It is also very funny." *–NY Newsday* [2M, 2W] ISBN: 0-8222-1698-1

★ **COLLECTED STORIES by Donald Margulies.** From Obie Award-winner Donald Margulies comes a provocative analysis of a student-teacher relationship that turns sour when the protégé becomes a rival. "With his fine ear for detail, Margulies creates an authentic, insular world, and he gives equal weight to the opposing viewpoints of two formidable characters." *–The LA Times* "This is probably Margulies' best play to date ..." *–The NY Post* "... always fluid and lively, the play is thick with ideas, like a stock-pot of good stew." *–The Village Voice* [2W] ISBN: 0-8222-1640-X

★ **FREEDOMLAND by Amy Freed.** An overdue showdown between a son and his father sets off fireworks that illuminate the neurosis, rage and anxiety of one family – and of America at the turn of the millennium. "FREEDOMLAND's more obvious links are to *Buried Child* and *Bosoms and Neglect*. Freed, like Guare, is an inspired wordsmith with a gift for surreal touches in situations grounded in familiar and real territory." *–Curtain Up* [3M, 4W] ISBN: 0-8222-1719-8

★ **STOP KISS by Diana Son.** A poignant and funny play about the ways, both sudden and slow, that lives can change irrevocably. "There's so much that is vital and exciting about STOP KISS ... you want to embrace this young author and cheer her onto other works ... the writing on display here is funny and credible ... you also will be charmed by its heartfelt characters and up-to-the-minute humor." *–The NY Daily News* "... irresistibly exciting ... a sweet, sad, and enchantingly sincere play." *–The NY Times* [3M, 3W] ISBN: 0-8222-1731-7

★ **THREE DAYS OF RAIN by Richard Greenberg.** The sins of fathers and mothers make for a bittersweet elegy in this poignant and revealing drama. "... a work so perfectly judged it heralds the arrival of a major playwright ... Greenberg is extraordinary." *–The NY Daily News* "Greenberg's play is filled with graceful passages that are by turns melancholy, harrowing, and often, quite funny." *–Variety* [2M, 1W] ISBN: 0-8222-1676-0

★ **THE WEIR by Conor McPherson.** In a bar in rural Ireland, the local men swap spooky stories in an attempt to impress a young woman from Dublin who recently moved into a nearby "haunted" house. However, the tables are soon turned when she spins a yarn of her own. "You shed all sense of time at this beautiful and devious new play." *–The NY Times* "Sheer theatrical magic. I have rarely been so convinced that I have just seen a modern classic. Tremendous." *–The London Daily Telegraph* [4M, 1W] ISBN: 0-8222-1706-6

DRAMATISTS PLAY SERVICE, INC.
440 Park Avenue South, New York, NY 10016 212-683-8960 Fax 212-213-1539
postmaster@dramatists.com www.dramatists.com